Just Battlin' On Regardless

By Phil Sheather

Copyright © 2020 by Phil Sheather

All rights reserved. No part of this publication may be reproduced, distributed or transmitted in any form or by any means, including photocopying, recording, or other electronic or mechanical methods, without the prior written permission of the publisher, except in the case of brief quotations embodied in critical reviews and certain other noncommercial uses permitted by copyright law. For permission requests, write to the publisher, addressed "Attention: Permissions Coordinator," at the address below.

Phil Sheather C/- Intertype
Unit 45, 125 Highbury Road
BURWOOD VIC 3125
www.intertype.com.au

Page layout and cover design by Intertype Self-Publishing Support Services

Ordering Information:
Quantity sales. Special discounts are available on quantity purchases by corporations, associations, and others. For details, contact the "Special Sales Department" at the address above.

Just Battlin' On Regardless / Phil Sheather —1st ed.
ISBN 978-0-6450010-0-6

This book is dedicated to:

My daughter Julianne, for her loyalty, devotion and support.
To my true and trusted friend, without whose persuading, this book may never have been printed.
To my late nephew David, whose infectious enthusiasm for, and appreciation of, my writings I found inspiring.

I'd like to thank my niece Suzanne Bredin, From Coolamon. NSW, for the cover drawing

Contents

Big Al 5

What Next? 7

There Is A Bunyip Down The Well 10

The Party Line 12

The Lamb Markers 14

Spontaneous Recall 17

Full Circle? 20

Shycosky Remorse 23

Ed's Black Eye 26

Mum's Turkeys 28

Wake Up Dad! 31

There's A Bible In The Hall 40

The Young Header Driver 42

The Drought 45

I Joined The Dole Queue 48

The Cockies Rouseabout 50

He Sang Tenna 52

I'm Gonna Git Me Some Silage – Next year! 57

My Hometown 64

Roundabout Rogues 67

Who Wants To Be A Farmer? 69

Not On Your Nelly – Mate! 72

The World Of A Mortal 76

Natures Stage 79

The Fox Hunt 82

Dee Cee 85

My Heritage 87

The Human Nav-Scan 89

Another Day – Another Hope! 91

Christmas In Hospital 97

The Cockies Header 100

Lost Youth 102

Ode To Roey 105

Cricket Trials 108

People In The Mall 110

The Cowabbie Cup 112

Harry's Son 116

Doc Harry 118

The Class Of Forty Three 122

Our Awesome Lord 125

Gifts And Talents 128

Lord, We Heard You Calling! 130

All Aboard For Twenty Twenty 133

Enforced Isolation 135

The Country Lamb Market In The Fifties 138

And I'll Think To Myself, What A Wonderful Day 141

My Emmaus Walk 144

Wen Oi Wos Yung 146

Volunteers 148

Grong Grong Sheep Sale 150

The Nomadic Enigma 152

Derby 154

The Spotlight Shooters 156

The Bidgee Flood 158

Perty Cat 160

Yeah, I Can Remember 164

Grace And Understanding – Where Art Thou Gone? 167

Women Of Distinction 169

Seek Ye The Grace Of God 171

Yesteryear 173

The Food Chain 176

The Trappers 179

The Evolution Of Youth 182

Stubble Reduction 184

God – Our Leader 186

The True Meaning Of Christmas 189

Our Anninersary 191

The Emmaus Team 193

The Apprentice Sheaf Turner 195

Big Al

If he knocks upon your door ignore all sense and rhyme,
And your status – be it professional or engaged in daily grime,
Whether rich or poor, clever, witless there's nothing now will save,
Cos your prospects have grown dimmer, and your future's very grave!

Because when Alzheimer calls he's there to rule supreme,
He'll strip away most skills and you'll find it hard to deem,
And then the fate of this once warm and beautiful soul,
Will be cast forthwith into a pitch black bottomless hole!

He'll use stealth and subtlety as his tools of trade,
And he'll not rush you – for fear you'll grow afraid,
Cos he needs you strong healthy fit and hale,
But once he has you hooked – well that's another tale!

He'll assume control and his dominance will commence,
As he removes some faculties including common sense,
He'll build your ego til you're a super human being,
The boss of all and sundry within your field of seeing!

Yet we'll get a glimpse of the wonderful person you were,
But it'll be transient – and more often than not – a mere blur.
You will retain your feelings and require our doting love,
But you will not comprehend – not even our Lord above.

You will become very adept at imparting abuse,
And may say – 'you have never been of any practical use',
Tis then we must focus on the loving person we married,
Cos deep down, you'll be the same, tis simply fate, miscarried.

You may throw punches as you succumb to being physical,
And expose family harmony to the point of almost critical.
Those who care will soon learn how and when to duck,
But will yearn for times of yore, and reflect upon your luck.

Now and then your discernment will be rendered unstable,
You'll believe you can perform chores you're totally unable.
Tis then we must appease you – often ignoring the true ethic,
Cos we're dealing with emotions that have sadly grown pathetic!

If aware you'd be horrified and would totally abhor,
The things you do and say, like stuff you'd never done before.
And it'll be hard on your family with your disposition changed,
And your common sense and sanity so seemingly estranged.

You will rarely smile but when you do it'll be like a bolt of light,
It'll lift the dullest moment and transform it oh so bright,
It'll bring back shades of yesterday that will seem so long ago,
Then suddenly – it's gone, and sadness, again begins to grow.

Yes, plan your retirement, and joining those ranks of old timers,
But add a rider, lest there's a knock on your door from Alzheimer's.
Cos you'll be blessed indeed if he chooses to pass you by,
It'll then be time to thank the Lord – right to the day you die!

What Next?

Far beyond that distant horizon,
That's where I was born.
It was there I spent my early up-risin',
And found my infant thread,
To life's maturity,
It was there I enjoyed security,
And 'twas there I chose to lay my head.

It was there my youth became exposed,
 As I searched for my potential,
And all my peers were similarly disposed,
Cos all farmers were then essential,
And I loved the unsophisticated culture,
Of those engaged in agriculture,
And how others viewed us was inconsequential.

But then began a subtle change,
As technology reared its head,
TV telecasts came within our range,
With news we seldom read.
We watched as some events evolved,
Sometimes with the answers unresolved,
But our thirst for more began to spread.

Now this sophisticated style of news,
Was fast gaining its momentum,

And TV's were here for family views,
And if you couldn't afford you'd rent 'em.
They kindled a thirst for knowledge,
That was never before acknowledged,
And created a craze that will ever torment 'em

But we saw so many ads on our TV screens,
Depicting our farmers as the nation's yokels,
I don't know where the script writers had been,
But there were very few like that among our locals.
Perhaps they are some of our jingle beauts,
But I reckon they'd have sold a lot more utes,
Had they been more tactful in choosing their vocals!

Some say it's sad but it was bound to occur,
With our laid back style proving such a lark.
But many fine folk were incensed by the slur,
That our elocution fell short of the mark!
So we set about revising how we spoke
Man became Sir instead of just a bloke,
And we chose other upgrades on which to embark.

We began saying "Pleased to meet you I am sure",
Instead of our usual greeting "How ya goin' mate"
And we replaced bully beef and mashed up spuds galore,
With quiche and trendy stir fries on our plate.
We submitted ourselves to a kind of revolution,
By committing our intellects to a mode of evolution,
And all because our ways and diction didn't seem to rate!

It was a pity from whichever way you view it,
This eroding of our basic country culture,
Deprived of our identities – but I guess we always knew it,

That our customs would be devoured by this insidious phantom vulture,
It has been a real tragedy in the making,
And we sat by while our heritage was undertaking,
This transformation alien to those engaged in agriculture.

It was always our tradition to stop and help a fellow driver,
If while on the by-ways his motor became de-chugged.
Now-a-days there's a risk you could be stopping for a conniver,
And a fair chance you could end up getting mugged!
But that's the price we pay for our progression,
And we either pay that price or cower in our regression.
Cos if we rebel the chances are we'll wind up being jugged!

We chose a PM who lacked culture and decorum,
And had the notion it was cool and smart to curse!
He had his aides place a mirror right before 'em,
To choreograph his eyebrows! And long did they rehearse!
Now both genders of our youth are daily swearing,
It's become a custom – just like the clothes that we are wearing!
It's a PM's legacy our nation simply can't reverse!
I often travel beyond that horizon and chat with friends,
Many haven't changed a bit and still cherish our older culture.
But our kids are different and embrace these modern trends,
And seize our traditions and shred 'em through a mulcher.
Now old fogies like me are left with quite an alarming thought,
Regarding the changes this modern technology has wrought,
In fifty years time, what sort of producers, will there be in agriculture?

There Is A Bunyip Down The Well

About a hundred metres from the rear of our home,
By the side of a creek sunk five metres deep in the loam,
You will find a brick lined water well.
It's been very reliable during many a drought,
And has watered thousands of stock without a doubt,
But it is also the home for a refugee from hell!

My Mum and Dad told me and it gave me a heck of fright,
And would they say such a thing if it wasn't totally right?
They said "Don't go near the well cos a Bunyip lives down there,
And it preys on little boys like you,
And it will take little Reggie too!
(Now just between you and me it gave us a terrible scare)

But me and my brother were as game as old Ned Kelly,
And we snuck up on that little old well and lay there on our belly.
We peeked o'er the rim and saw three naked hares down at the bottom.
So we jumped to our feet and sped like the wind to save our skin,
We ran to our Mum and told what we saw down there within.
And she replied "I'll bet they got too close and the Bunyip up and got 'em!"

So no longer did my brother and I,

Have that urgent need to espy,
Or pursue our fascination where the bricked in water was welling.
But it became very disturbing to say the least,
How the habitat grew for that Bunyip beast,
As it began stalking prey beyond its habitual dwelling

Cos you see – my Mother would often say to me,
(And who could be more concerned than she?)
That if I didn't do this or that the Bunyip would come and get me!
It had a say in all the meals I ate,
And even if and when I could stay up late
Now growing up's enough without that beast trying to upset me!

But I knew there was something not quite right,
(After I'd recovered from my initial fright)
When I saw three hare skins pegged out to dry in our shed!
I knew they were not put there by a beast from hell,
And as turned out my Dad put those hares down the well,
To deter us kids from loitering cos we wouldn't heed a word they said.

Well – my parents used a bit of psychology
And mixed it with a little mythology,
And between them evolved a plan that really worked out swell,
In retrospect it was a pretty good ruse,
Perhaps exposed to over use,
But it severed our infatuation with the water down the well!

The Party Line

"Will you shut up and listen – was that our ring?"
We were helping our Mother to garden and to do her thing.
"Yes that's our call- I'll go and answer the phone.
Now while I'm gone water the seeds we've just sown,
And pull up those weeds from where they've grown".
You see- we are subscribers on our local party line,
And our dial tone is a short, a long, and a short - by bureaucratic design.

Our designated number was a simple double one R,
And folk could call us from both near and far.
They could call us direct if they were one of us,
As a subscriber on the line they could dial without a fuss.
But dialling from outside was like a detour on a bus
First you dialled the Grong Grong phone exchange,
Cos only they could connect outsiders to our range!

Now our particular line was all strung overland,
And consisted of a single wire of just one single strand,
It was connected to a series of posts with proper insulation,
And the distant twixt posts was according to scientific regulation,
The lines trajectory was plotted after much careful consideration,
Following close scrutiny of the challenging terrain,
And the consequences of storms and flooding rain.

The subscribers funded and erected their party line,
And it was their duty to ensure it remained a hale and hearty line.
But despite planning prior to erection (and that was vast)

Huge limbs during wind storms were very often cast!
And when this occurred the line needed fixing fast,
Cos communications would be on hold pending an overhaul,
And the line only totalled about thirty miles in all!

Now lighting strikes could cause the phone to peel,
(But of course you would know it wasn't truly real!)
And if you felt an urge to eavesdrop and hear something new,
Just lift the receiver on another's call –they wouldn't know 'twas you!
You could hear their news and all their responses too,
But you'd need to be careful and keep your mouth shut tight,
Cos any little quirk may leave them guessing right!

And if you had news you wanted one and all to know, as a friend,
Just dial a scrambled code and invite those who answered to attend.
All those subscribers would participate in a telephone talkathon,
And yet be as comfy as whatever they chose to sit upon,
And if busy – they'd hang up and rejoin again anon!
There were no charges on internal chats so it was fine.
But now it's gone! And many regret the demise of that dear old party line!

The Lamb Markers

It was something to five when I rolled out of bed,
In response to our Father's warning,
And after we'd all been properly fed,
We moved out to greet the new morning.

Our task is to muster and bring the sheep in,
And Dad wants them yarded before the sun rise,
And that's the reason we did not sleep in,
Cos time is the essence with lamb marking ties

It was so bitterly cold on the frost covered ground,
With everything mantled in white,
And I'll swear the frost was still coming down,
As we yoked the horse in the morning's half light!

We mounted the sulky in solidified states,
Then gallantly drove to the mustering lea,
Where the dogs' pussy footed thru frost with their mates,
Tho their paws were encrusted in ice, they were ready to obey.

The field was snow white and the sheep had not stirred,
From the camps they'd made for the night,
And the dogs were off at the first hint of a word,
And the sheep stirred into action in response to their fright!

The field was still white but now had patches of green,
With steam drifting aloft from each smallish green bed,
Where the ewes in overnight repose had all been,
Ere the dogs roused their number of eight hundred head,

With the heat from their bodies melting the frost on their back,
It created an aura of rising steam in the air,
And as the ewes stamped their feet and charged down the track,
A bevy of small lambs spread out everywhere.

It took oodles of time and much of our guile,
With help from our hairy four footed mates,
Almost a full hour to move them a mile,
With the sun anointing the day as we closed the yard gates.

My Dad and elder brother were the 'surgeons' on call,
And they immersed their implements in a condes crystal suspension,
Cos hygiene was important to the lambs health overall,
And towards this goal they honed all their attention.

Now we lamb catchers were carefully drilled in the art,
Of presenting and holding the lamb on the marking rail,
"If it's a ram lamb be sure the rear legs are held wide apart,
And ensure the left ear is also exposed on the male.

Of course if it's a ewe then the reverse is the go.
But hold tightly to the rear legs and present the right ear,
Cos if you release a rear leg they can cause quite a blow,
So don't dislodge our implements and pollute all our gear!

We commenced quickly then settled at a steady rate,
But the smaller lambs allowed us to step up a gear,
And with the heavy lambs our speed would slightly abate,
But regardless the "Docs" were viewed without fear.

They were a couple of serious chaps, and had fuses quite short,
And they adhered to protocol – leaving all humour bereft!
But we had no caution and longed to put spice in the "sport".
So with two ewe lambs we called "rarm larm" and presented 'em left.

The Docs romped up with elastrators and rings – but no scrotum?
I know it was here we erred cos each of 'em blew a fuse,
And the language they used was foreign to us so in a coded form I'll quote 'em,
"A blankety ram is a blankety ram and the same applies for the blankety ewes!

You blankety fools are wasting time – and a change is urgently needed".
They threatened with their pliers and their ravings and rants,
So we vowed to amend our way – and the warning would sure be heeded,
Cos we were glad of those rails between us – and our tight fitting pants!

Spontaneous Recall

It was just by chance I met him,
And now I simply can't forget him,
Cos we shared so many mutual friends
He was a very easy bloke to talk to,
As we sat by windows we could gawk thru,
And chatted 'bout this modern era and its trends

We discussed the economy and rising prices,
As it related to modern farming with all its vices,
Cos we were both farmers not so long ago
We agreed the seasons have been torrid,
In fact for many they've been horrid,
Cos cash crops they simply could not grow.

Then our chat drifted to the growth of Aussie Rules,
And how it's now played in Sydney schools,
And he told me he follows the Bombers at APM.
He confided how he and his brothers played there,
And I remembered their brilliance and their flair,
And I recalled the times I'd even played against them.

He mentioned Tom from Griffith Swans –and his ungainly build,
Who played ore thousands and each he would have thrilled,
Tho the big fellow had a tummy like an awning ore his shorts!
But he had pace for the first ten yards,
With the ball his object – with or without regards,

Cos he would run you over without any second thoughts!

And we spoke about Bernie – who coached at APM,
Now he was a beauty – in fact he became a gem!
But I recall his slow start and how he even played reserves.
He was told, "It looks bad, Son, you're far too slow,
Pull up your socks or pack your bags and go!"
But he turned it 'round to gain the respect he deserves.

You've heard of foot and mouth? Bernie had foot and foot,
And when he got it right could that man hoot!
And he mastered the much aligned flick pass.
(Tho even today many believe it was a throw)
But the umpies turned a blind eye, or didn't want to know,
And as a result he became a member in the elitist class!

My old mate Ned from APM got mentioned in despatches,
He played a host of intra club and some representative matches,
But he was not fleet of foot and had a fear of elevation!
He liked the ball on terra firma – down there at ground level,
And when the game got a tough that's when he could revel!
And if allowed to get on song he was a revelation!

By and by our talk drifted into magpie territory,
When Wines and Matt were part of their company,
And Piep and Irish –they're still household names today.
When Big Bill and Barry Mac were all the rage,
And memories of their exploits continue down the age,
Before they stepped aside and made room for youth to play.

One of the things that can occur when you go footy reminiscing,
Is the ones that should be mentioned are often let go missing!
Cos you need time to release your memories and selective power
But it was a pleasant and thrilling exercise,

And my Mate provided me with data I did not realise,
So thank you my good friend – I really enjoyed that hour.

Full Circle?

There was some confusion surrounding the noise,
That finally awakened the boys,
From their slumber in the wee small hours of the morning,
Was it the result of my dream?
Did I awaken myself with a scream?
Each wondered hopefully, dreading the onset of a new day dawning.

But suddenly their Father was there,
Filling their hearts with despair,
"Come lads, don't make me call again, out now and go feed the team.
Remember, early to bed and get your rest,
And you'll rise each morning brimming with zest,
And besides, it will make men of you and build your self esteem!

Get to bed early and turn off the wireless,
Then you'll awaken regular and tireless,
And don't let your dislike of the Clydesdales be so obsessive."
"Dad, do you always have to be the actor?
Do us all a favour and go buy the farm a tractor.
Our production and profits will rise and the neighbours will think you're progressive."

But their Patriarch stood firm,
"There'll be no tractor acquisition during my term,
As Principal of this modest family farming enterprise,"

Now the years soon sped around,
 While the brothers tilled the ground,
 With the Clydesdale teams - amid the heat and dust and flies,

However, all eras have an ending
Despite strong wills unbending,
And their loved but determined Father slowly closed his chapter.
And the brothers two as his benefactors,
Went and purchased their first tractors,
After dispersing the Clydesdale teams in an atmosphere of rapture!

The two lads then plotted and planned,
Driven by a consuming love for their land,
And prospered beyond their wildest dreams and expectations,
They felt an urge for their farm to grow,
And purchased neighbouring land to sow,
And to graze so they could consolidate and prepare for the next generations.

Cos the brothers had wed and multiplied
And the Lord looked down and supplied,
Each with a son as an heir to carry on their family traditions
And their sons were given further education,
Cos there was no room now for moderation,
And the brothers foresaw changes and new enterprise transitions.

Their sons learnt all about computers,
And studied the ins and outs of the trading futures,
And how cash flows are important for the family farm's survival,
And all family farms are now numbered,
Cos there are very few left unencumbered,
And to survive they need careful planning to trigger a revival.

The brother's concern is their input cost,

And they watch hopelessly while their margins are lost,
So they consulted their sons who had done a multitude of courses.
The sons plied their computer with much data
And the answer it spewed forth later?
Your input costs have trebled since you farmed with Clydesdale horses!!

Shycosky Remorse

Young Shycosky Remorse,
Was a jackaroo shearer – of course,
But perhaps of doubtful repute,
He was a shearer of a sort,
Only half as good as he thought,
While his tallies he'd always dispute.

He was a shy kind of lad,
Not good – yet not bad,
Just an in between sort of bloke,
He would chatter away all day,
Mostly about nothing - I'd say,
With little truth in whatever he spoke.

He was no good at shearing lamb ewes,
Cos their teats he'd often diffuse,
And with wide combs he was a disaster.
All ear tags he'd up and disperse,
And the wether's pizzle he'd often curse,
Cos shearing was a craft he didn't quite master.

One minute he'd be your friend,
The very next he would offend,
With a Smart Alec backhanded remark.
He was an expert on human life,
Despite not having found a wife,

But on this mission he'd often embark.

He loved playing the fool,
But only by his own rule,
Cos the joke was always at another's expense.
He'd get surly and cursed,
If the joke was ever reversed
And he'd find it hard to constrain his incense.

He was almost twenty years old,
And still very much in the family fold,
With his father the head of the clan,
He dared not spend a mere cent,
Without his beloved sire's consent,
Even though he was growing up a man

He was a cranky kind of cuss,
And resented all the fuss,
If a sheep grew restless and struggled,
He'd turn crimson red and then swear,
And that was a warning to beware
His demeanour was becoming befuddled

And on the completion of that ewe's shearing,
He'd disengage the handpiece gearing,
And while seething he'd align with his boot,
Then take a savage kick at the ewe,
And if he missed he'd then follow on through,
And exit from the board down the chute

There both he and the ewe would be totally entangled,
He and the ewe were jammed tight and both dangled,
In mid-chute, (cos it was designed for only a single)
And the more they struggled and shoved,

The more firmly they fitted and gloved.
And needed assistance before either could again mingle.

Then sheepishly he'd return to the board,
Amid all the merriment as the rousies guffawed,
But then he'd manage to ignore all their jeering.
He'd then catch and return with a ewe,
And without any further ado,
He'd recommence with his shearing.

It was a rather sad state of ado,
For this handsome young jackaroo,
Whom no one could totally trust,
He was hell bent on being his own man,
And was totally immersed in his clan,
While he treated other's values and ethics with disgust!

Ed's Black Eye

I guess you've heard many and varied orations,
Regarding black eyes and closely related abrasions,
And I suppose many of those yarns can really test the limit.
Now I know you can get them in bar room brawls,
And some can result from simple falls,
But whatever the reason there's no need to inhibit.

Take for instance our very good friend and colleague Ed,
He got a beaut black eye and this is what he said.
"I just rolled out of my bed and hit my head on a chair".
Now that's a mild and simple explanation,
Quite feasible and not prone to exaggeration,
But one may ask – why have a chair placed there?

Now it's been revealed Ed often dreams of times of yore,
And 'tho only a dream he loves being involved once more,
And can apply his hand to anything while in a state of reverie.
This night he was chasing a mob of grey kangaroos,
(After they'd spooked his herd of Murray Grey moos)
And 'tho on foot Ed outsmarted them cleverly.

Now Ed is as fast as a hare and gained on those bounding roos,
As they crashed 'thru fences (And that was bad news)
But Ed did not falter and cleared them all in his stride.
He ran those roos ragged 'till they were ready to drop,
Right to the foot of Galore Hill and then halfway up to the top,

Where a big Roo turned and Ed growled "I'll have yer mangy hide!"

The big Roo glared and spat in its paws and rubbed 'em together,
And Ed decided the time was now right to go hell for leather,
And with a blood curdling scream he dived for the big Roo's throat.
But the roo landed a punch to the eye and a kick to the groin,
While Ed tightened his grip on its throat and kneed it hard in the loin,
And growled in the big Roo's ear "don't you dare look at me and gloat!"

Suddenly Ed awoke on his bedroom floor – with no sign of a roo anywhere,
And his hands were locked round the leg of a fallen chair,
And he was squeezing it tight (Cos his aim was to strangulate)
It then occurred to Ed it was only a dream and one he couldn't deny,
Cos it had left him with one leg of a fallen chair in his eye,
And he sensed a beaut black eye was now going to be his fate!

Mum's Turkeys

I would like you to go and fetch the turkeys, boys,
They'll be up the creek or somewhere thereabout,
And I want them home before sundown,
So they'll be safe when those marauding foxes venture out.

So off we set with our trusty dog at heel,
In search of all those errant turks.
And we tracked 'em for at least a mile or so,
Cos that is how a turkey muster works.

And I reckon we covered another mile,
Before we heard a distant turkey gobble,
Then around the next bend in the dry creek bed,
We spied them approaching fast and on the double.

We scaled the bank and counted all their number,
As below they filed past completely unaware,
Cos they'd wandered far and wide on their daily walkabout,
Before ending up in full view of a cunning fox's lair!

We dallied awhile for all looked fine and dandy,
And the flock was returning home direct and fast,
And they'd be safely home and roosting soundly,
Before the nights darkening shadows began to cast.

Suddenly our dog issued a ferocious snarl of warning,

And we saw two foxes joining in pursuit,
And we cursed our luck for not having brought our gun,
Cos we were both well positioned there too shoot.

So we sooled our dog onto that foxy pair,
(And we only needed one sic to get him underway)
Cos with one bound he was in the dry bed of the creek,
Clearly showing his eagerness for any pending fray!

Both foxes reeled back in great alarm,
Cos it seemed the dog dropped down from the sky,
But it didn't take 'em long to reorganise their act,
For have you seen a fox capitulate and die?

One turned and made a beeline back to the family lair,
And in what appeared a carefully worked out prank,
The other wheeled and sped across the creek bed,
In an effort to gain its freedom, by climbing up the bank

But our dog was fox wise as well as monkey cunning,
And you'd have thought he'd been and read their mail,
Cos he was barely a yard behind that wily mammal,
And as it reached the bank he grasped it by the tail.

He flipped it on its back in a show of brutal strength,
And then moved in carelessly to kill,
But with enthusiasm he'd thrown caution to the wind,
By ignoring the fox's cunning and evil skill!

The fox clamped its jaws upon the dog's left frontal foot,
And our dog responded with a yelp and mournful wail,
And when the fox thought it had inflicted ample pain,
It released the foot and fled only to be recaptured by the tail.

But this time our dog gripped it by its snarling throat,
And ignoring the painful throbbing in its pad,
He held his grip and shook the luckless creature rough,
Until it lay limp and lifeless in it's jaws egad!

He held it long and hard before he released his prey,
Then sat with one ear cocked and both eyes glued,
Upon that inert and broken lifeless body,
For any sign of life that may again be viewed.

My brother, dog and I were a very triumphant trio,
But alas! Somehow we must have raised our Mater's ire.
Cos we were charged with disobedient conduct,
And duly summoned to appear before our sire!

"Your mother asked you both to go and fetch the turkeys,
And I think that was a rather simple chore.
But in your wisdom you both went hunting foxes,
And your mother's mission you simply chose to ignore!

You're lucky those turkeys returned in time for roosting,
Can you imagine the loss if they'd been left out in the dark?
The foxes would have slaughtered every single one,
Yet – you treated it like some trivial daily lark!

Well – I've news for you my boys – your hunting days are over,
For the next three months or til you mend your errant way.
Now in the meantime your dog and I will be together,
And you'll get him back – only when you decide to obey."

Wake Up Dad!

I heard a guy on TV spruiking the other night about occupational hazards. And I thought to myself – you poor misguided fool. How misinformed or misleading can one possibly get or be! Look here– one does not have to be specifically 'occupied' to run afoul of a hazard! No way- don't you be fooled!

Why, hazards can actually seek you out! Just take me for instance. I wasn't even doing a darn thing, apart from virtually minding my own business. There I was enjoying a quiet little quality chat with my seventeen year old Son (my pride and joy?) The next instance (and I must admit I did not see it coming!) I copped a broadside of such a magnitude I ended up flat on my back (metaphorically speaking – of course!) and there I was, struggling to find my breath – and words to say. But not only that, I experienced great difficulty in just attempting to speak!

When I had partially regained my composure, I got up and dusted myself down (again -metaphorically speaking – that is) and sat down in my chair again, albeit with my bare face hanging out, but nevertheless attempting to look as dignified as possible under such trying circumstances, especially considering the magnitude of the tirade I'd just experienced.

And as I sat there, I felt like one of those three monkeys you often hear about – you know – see nothing, hear nothing, and do nothing? Oh boy, am I so glad there was not a fourth one called think nothing! Because I was desperately trying to think! Desperately trying to identify just what caused such a ruckus in the first place.

And do you know what? I eventually narrowed it all down to just one harmless, puny little remark. The broadside immediately erupted following my reference to – and I quote "you know Son, back in the good old days......" and wham bam! (but - no sorry Sam!)

My Son leapt from his chair like he'd been stung on the bum by a bull ant. He towered threateningly above me, and lambasted me with "For crying out loud, Dad, when are you going to wake up to yourself and grow up? The good old days indeed! They never were! Are you stark raving mad? Why, back then you had no TV, no computers, no electricity, no air conditioning, and look at the pitiful cars you drove, why, I could have out sped them on my skate board!

You had no skating ramps, no Big Macs, no pizzas, no cappuccinos, no discos, and everyone would be in bed by eight thirty. You had no life, old fella. How can anyone in their right mind call them the good old days? Just look at the schools you had? Many of you went to one-teacher schools! One teacher teaching up to seven classes! No wonder you are unable to comprehend just how underprivileged you all were!"

Oh boy! You know, somewhere along the way I found myself almost – but just almost, mind you– rejoining with "By crikies, you could well be right, Son". But something intervened just in the nick of time. I suspect it was my conscience. And I'll be forever grateful for that. So I continued to just sit there. I was still deep in the depths of my recovery, of course!

And I was sure glad that fourth monkey remained unidentified. Because I was still hanging in there, thinking. Thinking hard, actually! And I came up with one solitary word. Phooey. Yes – phooey to you Son! But of course he was well gone by then. "I'm bored" he had declared emphatically, and disappeared. Most probably ended up on the end of a Big Mac, or skating down the sidewalk frightening the lives out of little old ladies and enraging our underprivileged Mayor.

Under privileged indeed! Strike me lucky, these young ones of today don't know what on earth they are all on about! Their trouble is, they have come in at the top end of all of this new technological stuff and progress, and they honestly believe the present status quo is the be all and end all of life as they know it. They really believe all the brains that ever were and are, and are ever likely to be for that matter, are alive and kicking right here, right now, right among our present generation!

However, in the meantime, just let us take a bit of a gander at our so called under privileged existence without TV. Instead, we had a wireless (they call them radios today). And the wireless was an imposing piece of furniture in its own right, too. The one we had stood about a metre tall, and was powered by a wet battery. This battery was usually shared with the tractor or the car, depending on the required demand on either vehicle at the desired time of wireless usage. But usually an amicable arrangement could always be negotiated.

Ah! What wonderful times we had. Especially during the winter! We would all gather around a huge log fire in the lounge room and listen to the news on the ABC, and then tune in to Martin's Corner and Dad and Dave. And there was a programme titled "Count Down". As a child I always contended it should have been titled "Count Up", because it was a musical programme featuring all the latest hits, beginning with number twenty and working up to number one. But it was all wonderful music, and wonderful quality family time, where everyone contributed to the conversation in a meaningful way, appropriate to the occasion or the topic of the day.

I valiantly tried (but unsuccessfully) to compare those underprivileged times to our very present. You know, the family grouped around and watching the TV. All eyes glued to the screen – not a word of communication attempted. With often our Son wearing headphones and listening to music from a walkman, and watching the graphics on TV at the same time, and one only has to appear to be about to speak and the withering looks would sere your unshaven facial growth. Yes Sir, very unprivileged stuff indeed. Well, according to my Son's script.

Briefly, but just briefly, I slipped into that unidentified monkey mode again, because I was thinking of something my Son had said.

Sure, we had no electricity, no air conditioning, and no hot water systems either for that matter. (Ha-ha, I believe Sonny boy missed that one!) But did it psychologically scar us for life? Did it leave us a bunch of cringing idiots? No, not on your Nellie it didn't, mate. Well, at least it has never been officially diagnosed as having had that effect. Well, not yet – anyway (But with all this modern technology coming on board, and superior brains emerging from our privileged schools, watch out amigos!)

The fact is, you never miss what you've never had, and we did not have a yardstick to compare what-ever we had, against. You see, what we had, no matter how inadequate our present generation may consider it to have been, was in fact our yardstick. Everyone was, in effect, in the same bath – er, I mean boat!

We had a generous supply of wood on our farm for our heating purposes, be it for cooking, for heating water to wash our clothes or for our bathing requirements, it was all good. We had a Coolgardie safe to protect our foodstuff from the heat, and it was very adequate under most conditions. Not ideal, but very adequate. It was certainly not as streamlined and eye catching or as convenient as our current range of fridges, but our food intake was not restricted or contaminated as a result. We did not go hungry or suffer growth retardation as a direct consequence of all this depravation!

During the summer period we had large water bags to keep our drinking water cool, and providing one remained disciplined and ensured those bags were filled before retiring for the night, the water would be surprisingly cool the next day. And air conditioning? Well, we probably would not have had time to avail oneself of it had it existed back then, but suffice to say, we had a large sleep out attached to our home with roll up canvass blinds on three sides. On most hot nights, that compensated for an air conditioning unit, and we had the luxury of healthy fresh air to boot.

And about those pitiful cars? Oh my! I honestly believe my boy must be mentally deranged. (He probably gets it from a deprived Uncle or Aunt, should the truth be known) As for out speeding them on his skate board, I've seen those 'pitiful' cars negotiate roads with pot holes so huge they could swallow and digest a skate board rider and still be too deep for one to see it burp up his or her boots!

Okay, they may have lacked today's styling and comfort and economy, but they were reliable, those old cars. If they did stop for whatever the reason, then almost every man and his dog could tinker with the motor and get it going again. Just try to do that with these modern limousines! Why – my dog refuses to even look under the bonnet of the modern jobs now! But the bottom line still remains, where ever it was one needed to be, they got you there. How is the case going for all this under privileged bunkum now? Just what did we miss out on?

No Big Macs? No pizzas? No cappuccinos? No discos? No skate ramps? Always in bed by eight thirty? Oh brother. Who do you honestly think is under privileged here? Why, for a couple of bob you could get all the fish and chips you could eat, and, and mind you, get half a newspaper thrown in as wrapping! Many a good read I got that way. Where can you get the luxury of that sort of service today? Phooey – to you Son. And if you craved something a little more exotic, again a couple of deniers could have bought you a generous hunk of Devon or Garlic sausage, and dip one end in some tomato sauce, and you dined like a king. And if you still craved variation, you always had the old meat pie and sauce to fall back on for about a bob a pop.

And discos? Huh, who needed 'em? We had real bush dances and real fair dinkum balls that would turn today's young bucks and does green with envy. But, dare I say it? We had dance bands that turned out real music, music you could actually dance to! None of this boom crash opera stuff that leaves you trembling in fear and trepidation, and ears that seem to reverberate for days later. And all those gesticulations they carry on with – why we saved all those gyro antics and stuff for the footy training track, where all and sundry could not see you making a gawk of yourself. I tell you Sonny boy, you are flogging a dead horse here regarding this depravation caper. Try putting the boot on the other foot for starters. And if you need a hint, try your own foot!

I thought long and hard about all that school stuff too. Actually, I took a bit if a squiz from several different angles and weighed up all the pros and cons and came to some revealing conclusions. The foremost conclusion being just how darn fortunate I was to have been 'underprivileged' enough to have attended a one teacher school. But not only that, I honestly believe I was among the fortunate minority who was actually privileged to have attended one! Now why would I have the audacity to suggest such a thing? Easy one mate! We always got one to one tuition when it was required. (one on one discipline too!) With only a total of sixteen pupils in our school, our teachers were able to adequately take care of those chores when and where necessary. However, one of the big plusses was where those little ones just starting school had the opportunity to interact with every other pupil in the school, including those pupils about to leave. As a result, every kid was protective and looked out for each other. There was no need for remedial classes, no need for special self expression classes. Oh boy, could some of those youngsters really express themselves when and if the need arose! I reckon many of those small bush schools turned out some of the best well adjusted and successful men and women you are ever likely to encounter. They picked up all the values that really count, the values that helped Australia to become what it is today.

So again, I say phooey to all this underprivileged bunkum! I guess some of us undisciplined oldies could counter by claiming this younger generation today is grossly over pampered. And perhaps one could quote some supporting evidence to validate that claim. But the reality is, not all of today's youngsters are like that. Some of today's products are the most courteous, nicest and most responsible youngsters that ever were or ever likely to be. However, far too many honestly believe Australia owes them, and that they have rights! We were never taught that in our 'underprivileged schools'. In fact, we were taught just the opposite. The emphasis was always on what we could do for Australia, and what we owed Australia. So where does it come from? Have they been denied the basic requirements in life? That is, the sort of things that help make real men and women? Maybe, but then, how would I know? What with my underprivileged background?

You know, my pride and joy really got me thinking. (so much for that fourth unidentified monkey!) I actually got to thinking about issues that my boy did not mention, and in fact is probably not even aware of.

For instance, when we were kids riding our bicycles to school along a public road, adults would often stop and have a yarn to us. Yes, sure, we knew who they were, and there were certainly no sinister connotations to be attached to these little rendezvous. They were probably only interested in what our old man was up to, you know, how many lambs did he mark, how many bags per acre did he get, how many bales of wool, how many sheep does he run? Pretty basic stuff, really! Maybe they were just checking up on his version, because I'm sure he had already been quizzed on the subjects, I don't really know. It was a nice gesture but, and one we kids really appreciated. It gave us a feeling of being 'grown up', of being a part of the community, and yes, it gave us confidence, a sense of belonging. I well remember a few years later on, when I was a young man in the company of our local Stock and Station Agent and two senior farming identities from our district. We were returning from a special sheep sale at Lake Cargelligo, and before departing Lake Cargelligo the two elderly farmers purchased some water melons and rock melons for their family from a hawker's stall beside the road. On the way home, and seemingly in the middle of nowhere, we passed two young boys and a small girl riding their bikes home from school. There was not a home or school anywhere in sight, but there they were. The two senior farmers both exclaimed in unison "The poor little so-and-sos. Quick, turn around Dud and we'll give them some melons." And that is exactly what they did. Those kids were delighted, and were barely able to believe their good luck. We left them and they were still waving goodbye as they disappeared from our view.

This is just some of the stuff I have been privileged to have witnessed and been a part of, during our supposedly underprivileged era. Those sorts of scenarios won't happen today. They can't happen today, because caring parents cannot allow it to happen, not if they love and care for their kids, and certainly not with the queers we have in our societies today.

Back during those good ol.... dare I say it? No, I'll refrain. But during that era I don't believe we ever locked our homes when the whole family departed for town. And we didn't lock our cars while in town. Would anyone be game to do that today? Even when you leave your home securely padlocked, there is no guarantee you will arrive home to an unmolested house. In recent years we found it untenable to leave our tools and equipment locked in our workshop in our farm shed.

One day recently I was digging a hole to erect a strainer post beside the river on the river bank. Midday lunch time arrived and I had not quite completed the job, so I left the shovel and crowbar in the hole and drove home for lunch. On my return the crowbar was missing. The shovel was there, but no crowbar! I had a fair idea who may have taken it, and in time my suspicions were proved correct. And I can assure you, it was not one of those older underprivileged gents either.

Now don't get me wrong, I am not against new technology and or progress. Not in any form whatsoever. No Sirree. We must have it, and if not for modern medical technology, I probably would not be here today. And I actually attended TAFE College in an endeavour to master a computer. Now that was a scary experience at first. There I was, the oldest student among a brood of youngsters! But I got through it all. But even today I still don't trust the beggars! The computers I mean, not those youngsters! – They were all goodo bonzer, a really great bunch. They, the computers that is, always seem to be striving to take the Mickey out of me. Just like when I call the missus in so I can show off a tad and show her how brilliant I can be, and I proceed to demonstrate, only to have the smart Alec computer declare "You cannot do that".

That always manages to make me furious in a way, but yet I find it a source of amusement as well , You see, when I was a very small boy and just able to comprehend, I can recall my Mother telling me exactly that. In fact, I believe they were her favourite words because she frequently related them to me in various forms and applicable to the situations at the time. I guess that suggests she was a lady long before her time!

No, I'm not averse to progress and modern technology, Son, but do let us keep it all in perspective, shall we? I would really like to take the best of my boyhood era and today's technology and marry them together. But would they be compatible? Sadly, I doubt it very much. Because I believe everything has a sequence. My ancestors arrived on Australian soil way back in 1838. They did it very tough then, much tougher than we had it. But they were contented with their lot. And it was their era that spurned our era, and our era in turn spurned our present era, and so it goes on. We would not be where we are today without our early pioneers. Each generation lay foundation stones, or stepping stones if you prefer, for the next generation. If my 'underprivileged' generation had not been, do you think we would be as far advanced as we are today? Me thinks not!

Yeah – phooey to you Sonny boy. If I was underprivileged, all I can say is, I consider myself very - very privileged indeed, just to have been underprivileged!

Three cheers for those good old days, Sonny Boy!

Now having said all that, may I just add how much I am thoroughly enjoying myself right here today, and that I would not swap it all for quids. I am watching the test cricket on television, in air conditioned comfort, in twenty four degrees Celsius. The official temperature outside is almost forty one degrees. The only downside is, Sonny Boy is here, and he is full of the gab. He wants to talk all the while, and I can't concentrate on what the cricket commentators have to say!

There's A Bible In The Hall

There is a Bible somewhere out there in the hall,
And I've not heard it read since I was very small.
But I do recall some versus just the way my mother told,
And I'd like to hear them all again – before I leave this fold!

When I was young I used to really love the Lord,
But when I started school all that love I just ignored.
Cos I chose new friends and I did not need Him anymore,
And besides, all my friends thought Jesus was a bore!

So I grew up not needing Him at all,
What with my friends and me busy playing ball,
Tho adulthood brought concerns that needed organising,
But I seldom asked His help - cos I was good at analysing!

'Tho once I sought His help – and I knew just what I needed,
So I prayed that He would grant it – in fact I even pleaded!
But I might as well have yodelled cos He didn't do a thing,
And all I'd asked was for Him to pull a simple string!

Yet I'm grateful it was I who was able to save the day,
Cos I perceived all I had do was change my style of play!
The key to my dilemma was staring me the face,
So all I did was alter plans and the rest fell into place!

As I became established I didn't need Him any further,

And as I didn't need Him I avoided Him with fervour!
But I was haunted by that Bible and those memories did intrude,
And then I'd feel so sad and sorry cos I knew I'd been so rude!

But now I've grown older and I'm confined to my bed,
I've had the time to ponder on the kind of life I led.
And I often wonder! Did I accomplish all those things?
Or was God always standing by – and gently pulling strings?

Could you please find that Bible - it's out there in the hall,
And would you read it to me? I know the prints so small,
And with my eyesight failing- I don't want to wind up down in hell!
Do you think I can still get to heaven, to maybe even dwell?

The Young Header Driver

I got the call but only for a day,
As my Dad was going to be away,
And a header driver was needed to keep all wheels a turning.
My enthusiasm was easy to gauge,
Cos I was just thirteen years of age,
And pride deep within my chest was fiercely burning.

My elder brother was the one in charge,
And on what I needed to know he would enlarge,
With epigrammatic finger signals to ensure I did it well.
Because he was driving the tractor,
And I was basically his reactor,
Doing what he commanded and in a way he chose to tell.

The header we had was a model HST,
And one of the earliest ones you see,
Where all the power to drive came from a very large cleated wheel,
Hand and foot levers finely adjusted the comb,
And a hand auger levelled the grain within its dome.
And I was its driver! – why – I could hardly believe it was real!

"What's the matter with yuh – have yuh turned flammin' dumb?
Get the flippin comb up before yuh block the floggin drum!
How many times must I tell yuh? – do I need to go through it again?
When I want the comb lowered I'll point me finger to the ground,
And when I signal up then I want to see it upward bound.

You would understand it easily if you only had half a brain!

If only he knew half as much as he seems to think he knows,
Surely he would have seen me hanging on to avoid toppling on my nose!
When I released the comb control the under draft pulled it down,
And I wrestled with all my strength to try and regain control.
Now there is a limit to the abuse one takes before it takes its toll,
And I silently vowed revenge upon that self styled family clown.

I know I should have more compassion cos I know he wouldn't dare,
Speak that way had it been our Father sitting there.
I know it's been a long harvest with all tensions kept in check,
And he found it quite a relief just to be able to rant and shout.
It can be a safety- valve, where you let everything all hang out,
And it's a way to let off steam as you strain to stay on trek.

Now when I saw this huge green thistle barely a dozen yards away,
A crafty plan in my thought process came hastily into play.
I knew my brother was blissfully unaware of my conniving,
So when the great burr did finally present,
I dropped the comb and in it all went,
And with bated breath I awaited the reaction of he who was tractor driving.

As it entered the drum there was a horrible groan,
And the header shuddered and then started to moan,
While my brother rose from his seat as if fatally shot in his squat!
Black smoke poured from the tractor's bowels,
And confusion reigned amid my brother's howls,
Then the header wheel skidded and all stalled – because of my fiendish plot!

It looked a sorry sight just standing there,

And my brother couldn't fathom how or where,
The drum became choc-o bloc tight with the green and spiky thistle.
It was jammed in tight and was not easy to clear,
As my brother pushed it there and pulled some here,
And bit by bit it came away til the drum was as clear as a whistle.

It was not funny and I know that now,
And I kept my distance to avoid a row.
And I would like you to know I've learned my lesson and it won't happen again.
But I found it hard to suppress a grin,
When I saw his hands with those thistles in,
And I thought – really, which of us only has half a brain?

The Drought

"We won't get any rain in April,
Or if we do it'll be late – 'round Anzac day,
But she's apples mate –there's no need to worry,
Cos we are going to get heaps in May.

Just look at the ants – they're everywhere,
And the springs are softening way up in the hills,
While the curlews are sounding mournful at night,
And the new moon suggests there's gonna be spills.

We've had no rain for the last four months of this year,
So there'll be plenty to come and more!
And that's only allowing for half of our annual!"
Prophesied the young farmer next door,

But the brow of the old farmer is furrowed and lined,
His last fall was fifty points – back in November.
And his dams are dry and the tide down his well,
Is at its lowest for as long as he dares to remember!

His fields are not worked yet lay arid and bare,
And huge whirlwinds are lazily traversing his land,
They drift sou-westerly in a casual spiralling motion,
Removing valuable topsoil with the dust and the sand!

He sold most of his sheep for little or nothing,

And was forced to send his cattle away on agistment,
And he carts feed and water for the sheep that remain,
But that has become a heartbreaking commitment.

All his seed and his super remain in the shed,
And his expensive machines are just lying idle.
He needs to raise a huge payment by the end of this year,
But all he has left to sell is his old mare's saddle and bridle.

His steed succumbed to attrition - induced by the drought,
But the farmer insists it was more from a broken heart,
Incurred by the death of his cow (they were raised together)
And he can't afford to replace 'em, even in part!

Their son has endured about all he can take,
And has gone to town to seek part time employment,
His forebears in their graves weep tears of remorse,
But what's the future? – no money, nor chance of enjoyment?

Their banker – with his eye on the corporate ladder,
Says only bad management could affect their additions!
Its plain inefficiency – and he may sell them all up,
Thus ending five generations of their family traditions!

3 Five generations had loved and farmed all their land,
And five generations had prospered and grown,
And those five generations had improved and expanded,
By harvesting what each generation had sown.

And now their family's destiny is up there for grabs,
Five generations of blood, sweat and tears,
And not one generation disgraced their good name,
Not one betrayed their heritage during those years.

Each generation paid strict attention to changes,
And each generation adopted those trends.
It's not methodology that has them on knees,
But their Banker's assessment cuts and offends!

But all this means nothing to the man in his grief,
"Why must it be me? – is it really my fault?"
Perhaps his son was right when he angrily said,
"The Banks only interested in lining its vault!"

When a drought settles your land and spreads out its wings,
May God have mercy on those in its path,
Cos many have tried to avert its foul scheme,
And there's many left floundering in its aftermath.

When a drought hits hard below a man's belt,
Why do the bureaucrats think they know best?
Throw them in where the drought rules supreme,
And see how they survive such a reality test.

No one has the right to apportion the blame,
Cos there are no scapegoats for the sins of a drought,
But droughts are a leveller and it's a well known fact,
If you survive – you'll be tougher, for the next bout.

I Joined The Dole Queue

As you approach the entrance the auto doors slide open,
Cos they're user friendly,
The air conditioned breeze caresses your face – as you were hopin'
And the decor looks so nice and trendy.

I was invited to join the line – at number twenty nine,
Now I am in the queue!
A voice calls 'next' and a young girl leaves the front of the line,
And two more join in behind you.

Heads are bowed towards the floor and no one wants to chat,
It's going to be a long, long wait!
Is it the humiliation or the realization there's nothing to alter that?
So they just accept their fate?

"Next" and another leaves the line without a backwards glance,
And the thought occurred to me.
What if they said "next please", maybe our perception would enhance?
But I guess that will never be!

I saw a client leave, in tears, and another curse and called them names,
("Next" and another one slinked away)
There'll always be those with devious tricks ready to play their game,

But why allow rudeness to rule the day?

After forty seven minutes of waiting I was now head of the queue,
And I received my call "next",
"What can I do for you?" "I'm sorry" I said "but <u>I'm</u> here to help you",
And I handed him some text.

It was a fax of Austudy data for centrelink - mistakenly faxed to me,
And he said "No – that can't occur",
"Sorry – but is that your name? Well that's my number- surely you can see?
So just what do you infer?"

"Oh-oh that's okay, leave it here" – and he stamped the document.
But nary a word of thanks!
I was not bound to return it – but then a kid would have been left to lament,
Their attitude sorely ranks!

Are they damned if they do and damned if they don't? Sure, never be beholden,
But why all the power play?
An ounce of sympathy and a pinch of humility could prove golden,
And wouldn't it add more sway?

The Cockies Rouseabout

The Cockies sheep were in the yard,
Mustered for his annual shearing,
It's a time when shearers toil so hard,
And when ringers can be quite domineering

You have heard of sheds of fifty stands,
Where the conditions can be tough,
But a survey for average Cocky demands,
Suggests that just one or two's enough!

Some sheds are small and cramped for space,
And the shearer's sheep are communally penned,
Where the ringer with a sly and devious face,
Will leave the roughies for his friend!

But it's the Cockies rouse about who really earns his keep,
By picking up and skirting the newly shorn fleece,
And keeping an eye on when to pen up woolly sheep,
Then collect the belly wool following the shearer's release.

Sweep the floor and clear away the dags and all,
And when time permits press the fleeces tight,
And be alert and respond to any tar-boy call,
Then ensure the engine water level maintains its proper height.

A Lister engine is the one the cockies mostly used,

And it consumes a deal of water as it chuggs away all day,
It s the rousies job (so no one gets confused)
To top it up but keep out of the shearers way!

It's the rouseis job to count the shorn sheep too,
And record the numbers on the daily tally sheet,
Then apply the owner's brand to every shorn ewe,
And turn 'em out when other chores are all complete.

He is then required to brand the bales of fleeces,
(Bearing in mind they are yet to be bulk classed)
And then brand the bales filled with all the bits and pieces
(Cos the bellies and the locks are usually left til last)

When the shearing is over and the shed's cut out,
And the shearers pack their gear and bid hooroo,
There's still plenty to do for the Cockies rouseabout,
Cos he is the Cocky – but then, is that a surprise to you?

He Sang Tenna

E sang tenna in the church kwire,
And she sang sprarana,
E was skinee lika a peeza ten gage wire,
And she was lika iguana.

E ad nevva bin kist,
She sparked with anywun hoo cood gro wisskuss,
E wood nevva be mist,
And ees name is Elmer an ers is Ibisskuss.

E luvved er but didna hav the currage to tell er,
She oped e'd maka move.
But ow cood e – cos e was jus a shy feller,
And she was oh so smoove.

He growed eevan sadder,
An er art bled fur im cos she knowed not wot aled im,
An e knowed it an fell eevan badder,
Then she knowed e knowed it an thort the matta kwite grim!

Now she lived at ome with er Maw an Paw,
Wile e lived on ees own.
An she desspretly wanted to see im more,
But e was home alone.

Er art yerned fur im,

An she desided in er wisdum to do sumtin fur Elly,
E needed more vim,
She wood invite im ome an git sum good tucker inna ees belly.

So afta kwire pracktus she sed "cum on ome fur a feed?"
E kicked the dirt "er – orrite".
It was the kinda date of witch both of em wer in need.
It cood be kwita nite!

At the ome of er Paw,
Er Paw opened the door and sed "cum in lad",
An let im throo the door.
Now Ile mosey out an git sum grub wile yer chats wif me Dad".

"Do yuh think its gunna rain? The curloos ar kicken up a rite".
"Or – oi dunno" e sed,
"Tho the ants are gitten recluss and I erd an owl tonite,
Ope not fur oi gits tuh bed."

Wot teem do yuh foller ,
In the AFL? Sum fellas scem to lika thuh swons".
"Yeah – Oi bet me a doller,
Fur em to win on Satdee – Recun they'll slorter thuh dons."

"Biccy wilya say grace?" Paw ast of ees only dorter.
She umbly scd "Okeydoke",
An she sed all thuh things wun wood spect she orter,
Cos thats the way she spoke.

She sat necst to Elly,
An wen they acsidently tuched or she put er and on eez arm,
E terned tuh jelly,
An shivered an blushed an fal all funie – but suffered no harm.

Wunse she put er and onna eez nee (tho er Paw didna see)
An it woz warm an slim.
Elly neely carked it! Sum bred cort in eez gizzard an e slopped eez tea,
But – they safed im.

Er Maw then sed,
"Youse yungens go in an wotch sum telly wile wees clears up thuh table".
Wal – Elly wos now proppa fed,
So Biccy thort she wood make sum ay wile she wos able.

She sat Elly on thuh lowng and sat aside im wif e r edd onna eez sholder,
An e kinda liked it!
E rubbed eez edd and gradjelly snicked eez arm roun er – e wos gittin bolder,
An e wos yung an fit!

Den outa thuh blue – e kist er!
Wal – sorta. Yuh see – e rushed it an it kinda stuck on thuh bridj of er noze.
Necst time e woodna mist er,
Cos eez blud wos now throbbin an a warm felan corsed down to thuh tips of eez tozes.

E wood wate a little wile.
E didna wont to rush er – afta orl e ad orl nite – s'long as er Maw an Paw staid way.
Then e gives a smile,
Kinda like playin Rushen rulet e thort. But necst time thard be no dismay.

E gives er a tickle an she looks up an e smacks wun fare on thuh lips,

An she smiles at im.
"Oh Elly – I thort yude nevva do it – youse almos give me the yips, Waten roun fur yer yuh vim."

"O I luvs yuh Elly"
Wal – yuh cooda noct im down wif a fever so sprized wos e.
Then e gawks at thuh telly,
" An I luvvs yoe Biccy – but I nevva drempts yude eva looks at me!"
They wos kissin an cuddlin at a frisky rate wen er Maw an Paw appeered.
"Kwik Maw git me a buket of worter.
I reccon it orter cool em down" sed Paw – an although Elly wos skeered,
E sed "I wanna git itched to yer dorter!"

"Den yuh betta do it kwik lad!"
Worned er Paw. But acshuly, er pairants wer kwite delited.
"Yeh – I gess it aint orl bad,
Yuse can git itched – but blimee – yuh shore don't pussy foot wen yuh gits yersalf exsited!"

A cupla munths lata thay orl gits tuh thuh church an thays wer dewly wed,
An thays wer orl as appy as larry.
An at thuh wedden brekfuss it wos time fer Elly's speech and this is wot e scd.
"Oi nevva thort oied evva marry.

But oi luv Biccy an oi muss konkur,
Oive luvved er evva since wees wos nee-hy to a grarsopper playin on thuh villege riszerv,
An now oim itched to er!
An oim gunna werk ard at bean a gude usbin lika thuh wun she shorely diszerv.

An o cos thays ad a oneymune! Thays went afishin fer a week outa thuh bak o Berk.
Ther furst nite wos in thuh bak o ther liddle ol ute.
Wen thay waiked in thuh mornen, ashuman thay slept, e sez "wot a wundaful nite"- wif a smerk
"An oi nevva noed yude look so – er – sorta cute!"

Thays got up fer brekfuss seeryol an toest,
Then opt bak inna bed agin "Wees ar on olydaze" e sez "wees needs alla rest we kin get."
But the place thay seem tuh freekwent most,
Wos the bak o ther ol ute – an ther fishen lines nevva eeven got a teeny weeny wet.

Ayteen munths lata an e still sings tenna in thuh kwire an thay boff nevva miss a praktuss,
Cos she still sings sparana there,
Dispite thuh fakd she as a baby gerl in er arms an another cummen- an boff as shore as cacktuss,
Ittle be a boy – tuh maka thuh poifict pare!

Now e aint skinee no more,
Er cooken as fatted im up an eez growed intuh a ansum bloke,
An shez raidy-ant, yuh jus caint ignore,
Ow she kopes wif raren kids an luvven er man and cooken an, wal, orl is jus okeydoke!

I'm Gonna Git Me Some Silage – Next year!

Over the last few years I have watched interestedly, but in a non-committed, unenvious sort of way, the frantic swing towards the making of silage in our district, as opposed to the more conventional, and traditional, way of hay making.

Actually, over the years I have been more than satisfied with the end product that we have finished up with. In fact, I would go so far as to suggest that I have been secretly quite proud of the quality of our Lucerne hay. It has always been of an excellent colour, and has possessed a tantalising aroma. Really, I have often been tempted to almost have a go at it myself! Fair dinkum!

My two nearest neighbours, one on my eastern boundary and the other on my western boundary, were the very first to go for it. Making silage – I mean. Really, they were the pioneers behind the revival of the ancient craft in our district, were Kevin and Greg. With their very own modern variation, I might add. They are pretty progressive guys, and not bad fellas to boot, either! Anyway, I decided very early in the piece I would sit on the fence for a spell and watch until they managed to get all the bugs in the operation out of the way. Well, I guess I sat there for three or four spells, actually. It can be a darn expensive sort of an exercise, this new fangled type of silage making, if you don't have all the gear yourself, that is.

Our Local Bloke Agent at the time, young Harry, invited some of us more progressive cockies to a breakfast and a sky Channel programme based on the growing of pastures and their conservation as fodder during dry times. The compeer geezer of the video, a leading farm consultant some reckoned, got around to spruiking on making hay. Do you know what he had the audacity to suggest? He reckoned the best hay he had ever seen, made the way I make mine, mind you, was only suitable for garden mulch! What utter rubbish! No – not the flipping hay – his statement, pay attention now! Well – did that geezer get right up my nose! But of course, it was blatantly obvious that he had never seen my hay! I was not impressed at all, and confidentially, that was the main motivation for me sitting on the fence for as long as I have. And I would in all probability still be sitting there, but for the intervention of my beloved old Murray Grey bull, Ferdie. Ferdie in his own inimitable way, kind of brought about a mild revolution at our joint.

You see, we have a quality little Lucerne patch, from which we make our quality Lucerne hay. Well- where else? Anyway, it is securely fenced by way of an electric fence to keep our cattle away from it. Well, somehow Ferdie found a way into that Lucerne patch during the day, but always returned to his harem in the late afternoon. I got a bit suspicious of the old sod when I spotted him with that tell-tale supercilious look on his smug face after he returned one afternoon. He had this assumed air of royalty, and I almost swore he was as high as a kite. My heart sank! I knew and recognised those symptoms immediately. That was the exact same performance he always exhibited after he had his way with a couple of our heifers or so. Oh no! He had only just returned to my herd, so where had he been? I took a furtive glance in the direction of our Lucerne patch, hoping against hope I would not confirm my suspicions, but alas, the evidence was there for all to see. Sure enough, just through the fence in Kevin's place were grazing about twenty to twenty five of his prized Friesian heifers. The old blankety- blank had been with them, I was already prepared to wager our farm on it! The only piece of the puzzle that did not quite jell and had me a bit at odds was, he was still diligently and voraciously "running the radar" over his own herd. Where would he get all his energy? Of course, of course, silly me. The Lucerne! You know, just yesterday I spotted him even gazing lecherously at my grey mare. The sexy old coot!

So I immediately high tailed it down to the Lucerne patch and paid particular attention to the dividing fence between Kevin's and our place to see where and how the old beggar had gotten in. Kevin, I believe, would remain somewhat philosophical about the whole show. He would take it all in his stride, our bull among his heifers, I mean. He would be disappointed, mind you, but he would accept it. Boys will be boys, that's just how life is, he would say. But that young Bill, well now, he is a perfectionist. I'm not suggesting for one second Kevin is not a perfectionist either, mind you! But a bit of water has run under the bridge with Kev., and he is more flexible. (Don't confuse that word with supple!) But I really don't think Bill would see the funny side of it, assuming of course there is one! I reckon Bill would call for the supreme sacrifice. Blood! Ferdie's blood! Or even worse, from my point of view, mine. Maybe even the blood of both of us!

But to my surprise, there were no broken wires, no portion of the fence down, not even a single misplaced wire. It was obvious Ferdie had not trespassed on Kevin's soil. Strange that! A real puzzle indeed. And just to confuse the issue, I could not detect where Ferdie had taken one single solitary bite of Lucerne from our patch. Now my curiosity was well and truly aroused. Right there and then I made an executive decision to plan to scrutinise Ferdie's movements very closely indeed. And I did! Well, what is the good of being the boss of a joint and not knowing intimately what your constituents are up to? Honestly?

So very early next morning when Ferdie rather tentatively negotiated the electric fence (there was a short in the last panel) and entered the Lucerne patch, I was there! I had snuck down much earlier, and camouflaged in an irrigation channel, I had positioned myself where I could observe, totally unobstructed, all of Ferdie's exploits. Ferdie made his way rather labouredly towards the shade cast by a tree situated on the boundary between Kevin's joint and ours. Once there he continued in the same vein by laboriously lowering himself into a resting position, and then began chewing his cud. Occasionally he would flick his tail to discourage a meddlesome fly. And that in itself was puzzling, because the sun was not really hot enough at that point of the morning to unduly bother an ice cube, so why should he seek out the shade so soon? But I have to report that he remained precisely like that all day, excepting to move once or twice to catch up with the shade. And not once did he as much as glance in the direction of Kevin's delectable bunch of prized heifers! But then, when it was time for him to rejoin his harem, off he set. I had my field glasses on the old beggar, so I could detect every little detail, however trivial it may seem. And I must admit I was more than a little concerned, because he had that look on his face again! It was disturbing, because he had only loafed all day, and had no conquests to celebrate. All of a sudden, it became crystal clear to me! The old beggar was returning in anticipation of tucking into some more of our quality Lucerne hay! I know I am a slow learner, but even this should be sufficient evidence to convince that farm consultant So, now buoyed by the knowledge that our Lucerne hay possessed energy giving qualities of vast proportions, not to mention libido enhancing characteristics, I invaded our Lucerne patch the very next morning for the sole purpose to make more of the same. Ferdie had already taken up his self appointed position under the tree when I arrived, so I went ahead as planned and commenced mowing. There was a slight easterly breeze gently drifting across the paddock and it was gently caressing my face as I kicked off. But I had barely covered a hundred meters before my nostrils were assaulted with a truly delightful aroma, and believe you me, they were well and truly tantalised. As I was almost directly down -wind from Ferdie, my first impulse was to lay the blame at his feet – er – well, whatever. But by crikies, the old beggar had never smelt so delectable before, so I immediately dismissed the thought. And then it hit me, of course, my Lucerne hay! When, or will, I ever learn? By the time I had negotiated the end of the paddock, I knew for sure it was not Ferdie. Even he could not possibly be full of that much wind! So I merrily continued on my way until I was directly opposite my starting point, and had to actually mow around the old progenitor under his tree. I mentally noted his inebriated like condition (which is odd for a bull) but not only that, I was intrigued by the aura of indifference that seemed to have engulfed him. Yep, too much Lucerne hay for sure. I made another executive decision right there and then to cut back on his hay rations. Obviously he was getting too much of a good thing.

Suddenly I became aware the aroma had become much stronger, almost intoxicating. I glanced in what I believed to be the direction of its origin, and found myself looking directly at row after row of Kevin's silage. All tightly compacted and poly wrapped. Yep, I mentally conceded, it sure smells great, but only time will tell if it can compete with my hay! I continued on mowing blissfully ignorant of the consequences of the avalanche about to beset me, for another hundred meters or so, and then the penny finally dropped!

I simultaneously hit the clutch and the brakes, as my tractor and mower came to an unceremonious and abrupt halt. I know I was visibly shaken, and I took a little time to regain my composure. When the full realisation of my comprehension of the situation finally hit home, it was, like - soul shattering. Just the mere fact that it was not my Lucerne hay wreaking the entire seemingly miraculous phenomenon surrounding Ferdie, was in itself potentially stressful. But it now appeared inevitable that Kevin's silage was solely responsible for Ferdie's state, for his occupancy on cloud nine. And the old beggar had only sniffed it! And look how it has utterly rejuvenated him? What if he actually got to eat some of it? The possibilities were mind boggling. Two hundred percent calving rates? The possibilities are mind...... oh yeah, I've already covered that angle.

Although still a little shaken at the full revelation of the situation, I set my machinery in motion again, and even though deep in thought, I again began mowing. Round after round after round, in complete silence from yours truly. The further I progressed into the paddock, the more determined I became. Yep, the time had definitely arrived for me to git me down from that fence, and git me some of that silage, next year! Yes siree, and I must confess I became a little emotional about it all. I reckon it was the relief from sitting on that fence and debating should I or not, and my determination to prove that consultant geezer wrong. And now that the decision was out of my hands, I felt tremendously liberated. I felt I just had to express my feelings in some way, so I broke into song. I sang several of my old favourites, and then had a bash at a couple of the more modern ones, but I must admit that some of their complicated lyrics proved a little much, even for my vast repertoire. And then I had a crack at a couple of those ever popular arias. It was strange though, for some reason Ferdie departed for his harem much earlier than normal. I guess it was the noise from the tractor that disturbed him.

For the first time in my life, I was quite disappointed when I completed mowing the patch. However, I was up before daybreak next morning, but, and only too eager to get out and rake it. My Missus queried the urgency, pointing out that I had never so much as hinted at the importance to do so previously. Fortunately, from a marital perspective, any pre-conceived notions she may have arrived at to support a theory that I may be straying, were quickly dispelled by my mood when I arrived home at night. I found myself quite amorous – in fact I surprised even myself. And that set me wondering too. Wondering about the prowess of a couple of my younger married neighbours in this department. Both have notched up a few runs. You know, I have a strong suspicion there could be some sort of correlation here!

Anyway, it was about this time I became aware that I was becoming addicted to this silage. Not only in my desire to acquire some next year, but actually physically addicted to its aroma. Just like Ferdie before me had. Now I am not a drinking man, but I reckon anyone hell bent on becoming inebriated can actually do it on the cheap, and it would be much less stressful too boot. I'll wager you can do it by joining old Ferdie under that tree, and inhale some of the silage aroma. I'll further guarantee you'll wind up as tipsy as a monkey. And the upside to that exercise is, you won't get a hangover, and it is not going to cost you a single brass razoo. Come to think of it, I wonder now, do you reckon that consultant geezer could be addicted to it? It sure would explain a lot. But fair is fair, we'd better give the poor joker a break. I just have a feeling he is really on to something. His assessment of silage appears to be spot on, so maybe some of his others claims are not that far short of the mark either.

Oh yeah, I'm gonna git me some of that silage, next year! Mind you, I may have to make a few minor adjustments. For starters, I'm going to have to closely monitor the addiction angle. But even more importantly, I am going to have to isolate my old grey mare from that old beggar Ferdie!

My Hometown

Grong Grong, oh what a wonderful place!
(And I speak about the nineteen fifties town)
Where the residents exerted at three quarter pace,
And stress was virtually unknown.
It had fifty one homes thus far,
With twenty five without a car,
Cos funds to purchase were still being grown

What a wonderful place to be alive,
Everyone treated peers like their own,
And they would strive to help them all survive.
A place where no one was left alone,
Cos it was a close knit little community,
So full of compassion and unity,
And best of all they were all home grown.

The citizens were happy and self contained,
They enjoyed dances and sports and picture shows,
And you rarely heard if any complained,
About cultural plays run by the visiting pros.
In summer they swam nearly every week end,
At a popular spot down at Wright's Bend.
Grongy – that's where they wanted their kids to grow.

They had a pub and a bank and a butcher and all,
And three stores to ensure they were fed,
Plus three garages and a school and a hall,
And the train would deliver their daily bread.
A fully staffed post office with postal amenity,
And fields for all sports- as well as a cemetery.
There was nowhere else they'd rather be instead.

Yet – there were some lost opportunities,
Cos jobs were few and the pay was light.
You could lose your job cos of no immunities,
And the lack of transport was their biggest plight.
One had to leave home if they wished to advance,
And to many that appealed like a hole in the pants,
And they resisted it with all their heart and might.
But times move on and children mature,
And there was a revolution in the economy.
Fortunes changed and jobs grew fewer,
As the future became tough in agronomy.
Salaries rose for those in employment,
And accumulating funds found a new deployment,
Like cars! –the start of the towns inevitable agony.

Cars loosen the shackles of those constrained,
And extra cash can revolutionise their fate.
Soon they travel away to be entertained.
And sealed roads will further liberate.
They visit towns where they have never shopped before,
And buy wares that are cheaper than in their home town store.
And all too soon the inevitable is easy to evaluate.

The Stock and Station Agents were the first to nail up their door,
Their clients sought the benefits of larger city sales.
Then the picture show closed down and didn't function any more,

There was no viability in showing to a few lonely males.
The Post Office services were the very next to go,
Then the bank pulled out cos its business wouldn't grow.
And the daily train was removed from off the rails.

The butcher closed his doors and wasn't seen again,
And two garage proprietors gave up the ghost as well.
The pub and school and one store they've managed to retain,
But then the regular dances entered a recessive spell.
The trend spreads throughout the country, while we sophisticate,
And a return to those carefree days would force us all to suffocate.
Cos as a progressive society, we must always play the swell!

We've had similarities before and it will bring no harm,
Horse teams went but tractors replaced them well,
And neighbours will sell and neighbours will buy their farm,
(So the population shrinks! But on this we will not dwell!)
But never fear, it is all in the name of progress,
As we move forward may our communities not suffer regress.
So forward ladies and gents, and no one, please – rebel!

Roundabout Rogues

Within a herd of cattle at least one will be a rogue,
(And it's the same at roundabouts with some drivers now in vogue)
Cos where I live there's a roundabout close by,
And when I reverse into that busy street,
Some of the strangest drivers I often seem to meet.
Their language tests my humour and there's no need to wonder why.

I wait for a motorist to signal they're going left or right,
And pray they honour the promise and not cancel halfway thru' their flight.
Then I proceed to reverse (with just a chance I may survive)
They roar like a bull tho they indicated this was where they would not be,
They pore the ground and snort 'how dare you challenge me!'
Some Mother's do have them, butI don't know how they stay alive!

One day I watched a lady indicate she would turn to her right,
(From an outside lane and I knew someone was about get a fright!)
Now I ask- is this called modern lateral thinking?
Cos then like a rouging heifer she joined the inside lane,
And the bloke behind braked hard to avoid causing any pain,
Then off she roared leaving the smell of burning rubber stinking.

Now one of the approaching lanes is a left turn only lane,
But rogues use it to overtake before returning to the main,
And as they over take you're cut off as they pass.

Y'know, when drafting cattle the rogues want to be the first,
It's the same with rogue drivers (they have egos that could burst)
What a pity both species lack that bit of common class!

Let me tell you 'bout the girl who drives on permit plates,
She overtakes on roundies (to impress her giggling mates)
She is like a rogue calf, tail up and charging into space,
Perhaps a racing enthusiast, maybe she's a fan of Mister Ingall?
But what if she should maim or kill while still so young and single?
Just because she can't resist the thrill of a motor race

I've studied roundabouts and the driver who use them,
And I believe there is far too many who abuse them.
But the rules are plain and are so easy to embrace,
So why can't drivers simply follow rules?
Cos they are convinced all others are the fools?
And cannot detect the egg adhering to their face?

Who Wants To Be A Farmer?

The rain was a Godsend, falling just in time for seeding,
And roundup negated the need for weeding,
He loaded seed, super and fuel and proceeded to the lea,
To begin planting cos conditions were ideal now to start
And this soaking rain had left him full of heart,
And he was determined nothing would get in his way.

Cos five years of drought can demoralise a man,
(And often it's the Missus who's left to hold the can)
So when a drenching rain occurs – even somewhat overdue,
And the time is right to 'inseminate' your soil,
You must be ready to go and not half way off the boil!
Cos it's then a sagging spirit you have got to renew.

He worked twenty two hours a day, saving two for sleep,
 Toiling like a dog that would make the unions weep
 Until finally his seeding operation was complete.
He had laboured long and hard holding nothing back,
To redeem himself and get his enterprise on track,
And he dreamt of paying debts from an account again replete

A good throw of the dice will keep the banks away,
(Cos no one can claim his land any more than they)
It's the rise in property value that gives him a legal base,
Tho the reaper from the bank has listed all his gear.
The writing's on the wall, it's very plain and clear,

Another failure will see him ejected in disgrace.

Every grain he sowed sprouted plus every wild oat too,
(But the use of old 'tiger' saw the oats shoot thru'!)
It was a start for which you'd almost trade an arm,
But it caused late decisions (some from the blue!)
Like –should we crop another paddock? Maybe even two
And if it's only good for hay then what will be the harm?

Steady soaking rains helped the crops do really well,
Exceeding expectations when compared to last year's hell,
A very fruitful winter but now all focus is on the spring,
  And the advent of drying winds or a late dreaded frost
That prey on tender crops they so often do accost.
(And to a desperate farmer that has a familiar kind of ring)

He got his share of winds and a couple of late frosts too,
(Causing minimal damage was the official point of view)
But his late crops turned out bummers and didn't quite prevail,
Cos eighty percent of their heads were a ghostly sea of white,
(And many of those withstanding got a nasty touch of blight!)
So he cut and cured and prepared those crops to bale.

He hired a local contractor to bale the hay up tight,
(Who used a moisture meter to ensure everything was right)
He hired a front end loader and stacked the bales six high,
And assessed the value so he could have it all insured.
(Cos if there were to be a loss he wanted a just reward)
He needed peace of mind and on a policy he could rely.

Well you wouldn't read about it but late one balmy night,
The stack became ablaze and glowed so ever bright.
Spontaneous combustion was the cause of its demise,
Caused by granule sap still lurking in the odd random head,

It was sap the moisture meter apparently hadn't read.
And caught all concerned completely by surprise.

It was a windfall for the farmer (tho' innocently contrived)
And provided an instant cash flow (ere his grain cheques arrived)
But that was just a foretaste of the many treats in store,
Cos the yield of his canola was the best he had in years,
And the focus of his barley were the grain laden ears,
While his oats were superb and he couldn't wish for more

But the revenue from his wheat put the icing on the cake,
(Out yielding other commodities as it left them in its wake)
It was an astounding year and his look wasn't hard to rank,
As he wore this grin that stretched from ear to ear,
Cos he was still the boss (for at least another year
And he repaid a chunk of debt to the reaper from the bank.

The moral of this story is not that hard to see,
(And it applies equally to you and yours and me)
Cos when things get tough and worsen day by day,
You have to buckle down and give it your best shot,
Whether you feel like doing it not,
Then hope and pray that destiny will finally smile your way.

Not On Your Nelly – Mate!

I was born to parents whose blood came from good old farming stocks.
(One of six siblings, two prim and proper pullets and a quadruple brace of cocks)
And our Aussie heritage began at Camden back in John Macarthur's day,
Cos he paid our forebears passages for three years bonding of their way.

When he drew land at Nangus our forebears helped to run his new selection,
With Great Grandfather in charge of all the horses in John's equine collection.
And my parents got to know the value of a denier when it came to rearing kids,
Cos of the ongoing battle with Mother Nature while striving to earn some quids.

Mother milked a herd of jersey cows and separated the milk on offer,
Then traded the cream for dosh to provide a lining in their coffer.
She made the family's bread and butter and raised a flock of turkeys on the side,
For those days were long and rugged for a good old cockies bride.

She would sell the turkeys at Yuletide cos then demand would reach its greatest,

And the dosh received allowed her kids to be dressed in all the latest.
I've seen Mother stooking green sheaves with no sign of duress,
I've seen her high on a haystack turning sheaves with great finesse.

And my parents knew El Nino like some scheming noxious rellie,
Yet you speak of Cocky whingers? No way mate–not on your flipping Nellie!
El Nino is a cunning coot arriving when my parents needed it the least,
(And would hand them a famine when they were hoping for a feast)

It would start quite harmlessly and seemingly full of good intention,
But then events occurred like empty dams and no rain of any mention.
The grass and crops would shrivel as the sun eroded all their vigour,
And the stock grew lean and weak as the drought kept on growing bigger.
The dam waters reduced to a slimy muck depriving stock of their daily guzzles,
As they circled watering holes tormented by their parched and burning muzzles
They knew the danger but their nagging thirst made it so easy to relent,
And venture into the slimy depths and struggle til their energy was spent.

Then their weary heads would sink into the slime, and they would suffocate.
My Dad was ever vigilant but often arrived that little bit too late.
Any alive he rescued from the depths and hauled to safety so to speak,
But lack of food and stress wilted spirits, and most would die within a week.

'Twas torturous for all concerned cos both shared a common bond,
And real farmers have respect for their animals and can grow really fond.
Yet you in the comfort of your lounge room watching the drought on telly,
Complain about whinging cockies? Well don't mate – not on your bleeding Nellie!

Have you ever driven a ground drive header with a whopping eight foot chop?
Pulled by four horses cos that's all you need to harvest a stricken crop.
Just sitting there all day with the drum at a high pitched drone,
Cos the heads were sparse and not enough to cause the drum to groan!

The box held seven bags but it took three hours to reach this objective,
(You could count each grain into the box to put it all in perspective!)
But there were times when God smiled down with warmth and charm,
And the crops grew tall with heads all full (for which you'd trade an arm)

The rains would come and the dams stayed full while the stock were always fat,
The grass grew high, you'd make next year's hay and it's hard to top all that.
Yet they had no electric power but this they could ignore
But to keep all perishables fresh all week was really quite a chore.

With the temp a hundred and twenty where the trees cast shade at noon,

Then off to town with the horse and heat cos they had to be there soon.
The phone was out and the line was down 'twixt home and the phone exchange,
Now that was the life my parents embraced, with dignity, and pride on their range.
Yet you, with a stubby and cynical smile, viewing sport on telly,
Call them cocky whingers! Well don't friend, not on your doggone Nelly!

The World Of A Mortal

Can you imagine a world devoid of God's creations?
A Godless place where mere mortals reign supreme,
Where the Bible is unknown and its pages never read,
Where mankind sets the agenda with purely a mortal theme?

Well let us grant the world one or two concessions
To help the populace establish a sort of repertoire,
And with God's blessing let it be stocked with only humans,
As the sole occupants although I know it sounds bizarre

However as a base they'll need a piece of earth,
For a place in which to create their own society,
And from here on God's aids will need to be selective,
To keep this exercise free of divine propriety.

Let's disperse with lot of God's creations to give us some idea,
How much we take for granted as our life gets rough and terse,
And we're out on our own with no backup ere in sight,
(It'll give a clearer perspective on who runs this universe)

Can you visualise a city perpetually languishing in darkness,
And its streets full of pedestrians with no sign of any cars?
A city devoid of sun and warmth or an illuminating moon
Cos God's the Master of the sun and moon and stars

As you walk the cities pavements what would you expect to see?

Only the result of human enterprise as you fill your leisure hours
It'll be mortally inspired cos you won't see any trees,
For they are God's creation along with all the flowers!

May God grant these people clay to manufacture bricks,
So they may build homes with grandeur and finesse,
But they'll fail to create an aura without all the proper gear,
Like lawns and shrubs and flowers with which only God can bless

Do you think they'll miss the singing of the birds?
 And the stars as they straddle the milky-way,
They even may yearn for an evening breeze,
Laden with the sweet perfumes of early May?

How about early morning dews upon the grass,
And the sunrise as it filters through the leaves?
The comforting sound of rain upon their roof!
Without all this I'm sure many hearts will grieve.

And of cause they'll need a serious change of creed,
And forget daily showers and washing out their clothes,
Cos there'll be no swimming and they'll have to negate a thirst
Because God controls all water and without it they'll end up on the nose

An interesting dilemma will be the manufacturing of their clothes,
As the only available fibre will be their own human hair
Now what will happen if genetics cause early baldness to occur?
I guess there'll be a shortage with not a single hair to spare

And there's a problem with cooking whatever there is to eat,
Cos there'll be no knives, forks or cups and plates to use.
And roast meats and vegies will no longer be a treat.
And you won't find a menu from which too leisurely peruse.

It's going to be a rugged lifestyle for all to take on board,
Given all comfort ratings will be recorded less than zero,
'Cos they cannot use components created by our Lord.
And surely that suggests He's a special kind of hero?

And what about those who are crazy about their sport
I guess athletics is all they have to choose.
"Cos they'll have to delete the high jump and the vault,
And the shot putt and the javelin are a couple more they'll lose.

And annual vacations with all those countless trips away
It could be miserable if you like surfing in the sea.
The only option would be hiking in the dark,
But only after you trek to wherever you want to be.

And recording time to divide their work and play?
Will a human count the seconds and give an hourly beep?
And be on hand to indicate when anyone wants the time?
(But then they'll need two lest one of them falls asleep)

Now let's acknowledge our Lord and give credit where it's due,
'Cos the more one considers the more you must agree,
Our Lord created this universe and all within it too,
And besides, without Him, there'd be neither you nor me!

Natures Stage

I'm sittin' on me v'randah watchin' the summer sun creep down,
Behind a crowd of trees loafin' on the horizon of this scorched brown earth.
I often visualise trees as people – all nonchalantly hangin' around,
In one and twos or some in groups, chatting and chuckling with mirth.

Like humans they appear in all shapes and sizes and have individual stances.
You'll see fat ones and lean ones and some are short and others tall,
All clothed in tight fitting bark with diverse leaves covering their branches.
And the leaves vary in size and colour, some are large and others small.

I guess I could return to my television and watch a scantily clad sheila parade,
Now that may be stimulating to some but it does nothing for my intellect.
I reckon old age has grabbed me cos my outlooks rather staid,
 All this sex and drugs that's excitin' our youth – I reckon's circumspect!

Naw – I'll git me kicks by gawkin' at that naked ol' red gum tree.
She's naked orright – well its leaves are gone and its limbs are stark.
It ain't nothin' to write about and you'll never see it on tv,

But it's starkers - bare as a baby's bottom – completely devoid of bark.

Every summer arvo it fills with hundreds of gaily performing galahs,
It's the focal point of their watering hole and they come from far and near,
They fly in for a drink with their mates (like our fellas in their supped up flashy cars)
And they show off to their sheilas too (like our blokes after they've had a beer)

I've seen 'em bungy jumpin' from the top of that ol' gum- well it seemed that way to me,
I saw one flyin' with a folded wing –heh- he raised a few squawks but didn't git far.
An' last night one was on the high bars- well- a bare branch of that naked ol' tree,
Hangin' by his feet with his wings extended- til another pulled his tail feathers- silly galah.

For a change one was hangin' by his beak and flappin' his wings, doin a chinup,
That's how I saw it anyways. Yep- they sure are a crazy mixed up breed.
I'll swear I saw one flyin' upside down the other arvo- now there's a turnup!
Yeah – they are a bunch of fun lovin' show offs – but I sure like their creed.

Ever seen 'em doin' galahobatics? Like free fallin' from the sky like a stone?
Or zig-zag flyin' at dangerous speeds. Can't have cops else they'd be on a charge.

But one thing I'll grant them – they have rules. Pity we can't do a clone,
And fashion a human, but use their creed and morals, and then, enlarge?

They'd been partyin' and ragin' for two hours after the sun dipped into the spur,
And twilight shadows were startin' to settle when the shindig drew to a head.
A couple reckoned it was time to go- and bid hooroo as they winged into the fading azure,
Then others flew down and had one for the road – ere heading for home and bed.

As the full moon peeped o'er the ridges, the ol' gum was again naked and bare,
Yet for a time was adorned like a queen, full of vitality and vim and power.
It's white, pink and grey buds the envy of all and its peers scowled in despair,
How could a flippin' ol' hasbeen like that – resemble a beautiful flower?

I was sitting pondering nature and kinda thinking til well after the moon was born,
And the shadows began forming eerie shapes on the drought ravaged ground,
A bird alighted in that ol' gum, and enhanced by the moon looked so forlorn,
It softly called 'mopoke', it was then I pulled the curtain on that sad haunting sound.

The Fox Hunt

Mother lost three of her chooks with their clutches of chicks,
When they fell victim to a cunning vixen's tricks,
The fox burrowed beneath the fowl's wire netting enclosure,
Then subjected the inhabitants to an unholy night of exposure

This made our Mother extremely irate,
And filled her heart with so much loathing and hate,
For that vixen and the general fox communities,
And she demanded their demise- with no immunities!

She gave Dad an ultimatum and it was rather blunt,
"Not another morsel of food 'til you organise a hunt.
You go and seek and destroy that vixen and her lair,
And how you go about it I really do not care!"

"I've grown sick and tired of those foxy denizens,
Denying my chooks the right to live with the other aliens
Now get off your bum and find them, I'm sure they're all nearby,
Just go out and get them – at least - go and have a try!"

So Dad gathered the dogs and enlisted the help of sons,
And unlocked the cupboard and brought out his deadly guns.
And we set off to target a patch so thick with saffron thistle,
There was scarcely room enough for a man to even whistle.

"Your brother and I will take the guns down-wind to our position,
While you boys take the dogs up-wind, and be quick in your transition,
And when you arrive there make a noise and get the dogs to bark,
'Cos if those foxes are around that'll prick their ears and make them hark"

We arrived and got the dogs to bark (and we joined the chorus too)
Then soon after from down-wind we heard this loud ado.
Five shots rang out and the dogs pricked up their ears,
As suddenly from the thistle patch a lonely fox appears.

Our stag and sheep dog and terrier all began to chase,
But it was the stag that led the charge with his superior pace.
He was fast and bridged the gap and forced the fox to turn,
And then the fox turned again in a desperate bid to learn,

Just how to shake this jet propelled carnivorous hound,
Then it turned towards its family lair to seek safety underground,
The fox gained some ground with this sudden change in direction,
But then collided with the terrier 'cos it failed in its detection

he terrier was delighted as it latched onto the fox's tail,
(But got towed along 'cos its strength was of no avail)
But by the time the fox was rid of the gutsy little pest,
The stag was on the scene and he wasn't there for jest.

The fox fought hard but succumbed to its own demise,
And the dogs were ecstatic with their unexpected prize.
Dad and our brother had scored a bag of three,
 And found the fox's lair in that thistle infested gully.

We dug the burrow out and found feathers from mother's chooks,
And also half a dozen pups in a couple of its nooks.

We were able to tell our Mum that the hunt went very well,
And now the vixen and her clan were residing down in hell.

Dee Cee

I will never forget that day when we first met,
And he smiled a toothless grin from the depths of his basinet.
Wal and I were down the paddock stripping wheat,
His Mum and Dad dropped in while they were passing by,
And they were as proud as punch and I couldn't figure why,
Cos I expected to see an infant a little more complete.

He had a bald pate with not a sign of a single hair,
And a gummy mouth with no teeth at all in there!
(Why – we culled our gummy ewes when they finally reach that state!)
He had this wrinkled face and half closed squinty eyes,
And oh boy – was he a blooming real surprise!
Surely there were other options for his parents to contemplate?

In time he did grow a head of hair (but it didn't last that long)
He must have dodgy genes (or something else is wrong?)
Cos he is only sixty – and already he's falling apart!
Aye – he sprouted a set of teeth – but they are thinning out,
So one must query longevity (or could there be some doubt?)
Or has he gone full circle – and is now ready for a restart?

But he was a normal lad and managed to play some sport,
Albeit a poofter code (and that left me quite distraught!)
And he studied both types of figures (but then got certified!)

But now he's a business leader and hoists the flag of his craft so high,
And has uplifted the name of Connell, right to the heavens nigh,
Congratulations Dee Cee – you have every right to be gratified!

My Heritage

  It's funny in a way
How your thoughts just seem to stray,
And you will dream about your old ancestral home.
Yet it's natural I suppose
When you allow yourself to doze,
Past memories of your birthplace will incite your dreams to roam.

I often drop by to visit awhile
When my dreams and boyhood reconcile,
At my ancestral home by the Yarren and Dead horse Creek.
I dream of the great times we had,
And of course of some of the bad,
Then that past retention haunts me for the next ensuing week.

My ancestral digs look oh so stately,
When I drop in as I often do so lately,
And I recall those hot droughty days when we were young and foolhardy.
When the land was hot and barren,
Between the Dead Horse and the Yarren,
And the meat went off and the butter melted in the bowels of the old Coolgardie.

I've seen those creeks swiftly flowing,
While my Dad was deftly rowing,
To forde the floodwaters when the rains were tumbling down.

I've trodden on soil as soft as jelly,
And seen green grass grow to the milk cow's belly,
From the Dead Horse right to the other side of town

We had dust storms all pitch black,
They came in the front door and out thru the back:
And shrouded Sol in darkness for a couple of days at least,
Yes siree you had to pretty daren',
To live beside the Dead Horse and the Yarren,
Where your future teetered 'twixt a famine and a feast

As the years go by I sit and ponder,
'Bout those early days down yonder,
And my thoughts are fruitful with no chance of growing barren,
As long as I can visit in my dreams,
And linger around those semi arid streams,
Near my cherished ancestral home twixt the Dead Horse and the Yarren!

The Human Nav-Scan

"Now slow down – we're coming to a roundabout,
So watch for and give way to the traffic on your right.
Now it's clear – go! But indicate how you'll exit out!
It's simple if you concentrate and remain alert and bright."

She was a passenger in my car and seated in the front,
Where her tone was terse to coldly blunt,
Cos a spade is a spade in her vocabulary,
Influenced by past exposure to the northern constabulary

"You had better steady down cos the road ahead's unsealed,
Can't you read the signs? You're driving far too fast!
Just read the signage and all will be revealed!
Now watch what you're doing lad or none of us will last!"

She is deeply interested in events and times historic,
In fact some of the deeds she relates are really quite heroic.
And tho' many of them occurred so many years ago,
At the time I'm sure they set many hearts aglow.

"How far are we away from our proposed destination?
Have you any idea what time we are due on arrival?
Surely you must have made some critical estimation?
(Keeping in mind of course passenger safety and survival")

She is a spinster and at times can be really quite frenetic.

(I'm unaware of family history – it could well be genetic!)
But she's a kindly soul and possesses a heart of gold,
And always offers a helping hand (or so I have been told).

"There are raindrops on the windscreen – it needs to have a wipe,
And steady down a bit – there could be heavy rain ahead.
For heaven's sake man you'll give me the gripe,
Can't you see for yourself? (I'd be better home in bed)"

She's very well read – and quite an intelligent lass,
And in her age group is clearly top of the class.
But she's a little eccentric and very set in her way,
And that's a worry – cos it can lead to many affray.

"I see a flashing light ahead so there are policemen up the line,
Maybe breathalysing – so you'd better get ready to stop,
And don't do more than sixty or you'll get a hefty fine.
Now watch what you're doing - you never antagonise a cop!"

Ben spoke about nav-sat (and aid for motoring navigation)
And how it shows the way (and to her it was a revelation!)
And how it monitors journeys from a navigational satellite,
You just need to follow instructions for your trip to be alright.

"I'm not sure about that contraption – yapping in your ear!
Telling drivers where and when to regulate their speed.
A gadget spruiking wisdom? Why that sounds rather queer!
How can a driver concentrate and hearken – and be free to heed?"

Her response was a classic in the current scheme of things,
Cos she's unaware of how she sounds in another person's ears.
But she has other qualities that she can and often brings,
So let's be thankful for her presence and accept her as she is!

Another Day – Another Hope!

She is wakened early, but she knows what time it will be, even without consulting her bedside clock. She knows from experience it is that close to four forty five that the difference will not count.

Because every morning at this time a pesky little black bird begins to sing his heart , just outside her bedroom window. Normally she enjoys waking up to the melodious sound, but these last few weeks her mood has not been quite as receptive as previously. Because waking up means confronting reality, and confronting reality head on is not an enviable compromise to sleep, under the present set of circumstances.

Because the current reality is, she and her husband are farmers. Not just farmers per se, but farmers in the grip of one of the severest droughts on record. She drags herself reluctantly from the comfort and security of her bed, and optimistically advances towards the window to join her husband, who has already dressed, and expectantly peers out. It is almost too dark to discern if there are any rain clouds gathering, but both of them are forever optimists. She dresses quickly, and hurriedly prepares their breakfast, and it in turn it is disposed of in a similar manner.

Their financial position has grown to be rather precarious of late. So much so her husband has been forced to take an off farm job. Fortunately for them, their neighbour owns a station property of several thousand hectares, and his annual shearing is in full progress which has provided her husband with four or five weeks work. And the opportunity exists for him to join the shearing team for further work when this shed finally cuts out. However, in the meantime their farm and stock need caring for, and this is where she comes in. She has filled this role extremely capably.

Water for their stock is fast becoming the most pressing problem, although their pastures are getting scarce as well. But they are able to make do with supplementary feeding, and providing they can continue with this, they should last a little longer. But with five of their nine dams already dry, and only about two weeks water estimated to be left in the remaining dams, time is fast running out. Sure, there are alternatives, but they all cost money, and that is a commodity that is most conspicuous by its absence when one surveys their bank account.

Now out in the paddocks and attending to her chores, she checks the remaining water bearing dams on their seemingly God forsaken property, which is a ritual she performs first thing each morning and the last chore every night. Her heart sinks, for a cow is stuck in the oozing, smelly, bluish coloured mud of one dam. She fetches a rope from her ute, and removes her boots and socks and rolls her trouser legs to half mast, and then manages to affix the rope around the cow's neck. The ute is then manoeuvred into position, and the cow is slowly extracted from the unyielding mud.

The unfortunate cow struggles valiantly to get to its feet, but the effort expends all its meagre supply of strength and energy, and it flops forlornly back onto its haunches and then rolls pathetically onto one side. She wrestles with great difficulty to get the cow back onto its haunches and into a squatting position, and then fetches a dipper of oats from the ute for it to nibble on, only too aware that she is only prolonging the inevitable, and the poor unfortunate beast has Buckley's chance of ever recovering. The cow is shivering uncontrollably, because the night in the cold mud has taken its toll, and already a thick mucus is discharging from its muzzle.

Further discouraged, she continues on her tour of inspection, with whatever remaining optimism she may still have, being slowly eroded away.

She approaches the ewe paddock with the-feed out trailer loaded with grain in tow, and the nursing and expectant matrons all suddenly congregate around the gate, from all corners of the paddock. They form an almost impenetrable wall around the entrance. Their hungry bleating is most deafening. Somehow she manages to get the ute and trailer through the gate without any sheep exiting the paddock, and lays a trail of precious grain among the loose dirt and dust on the ground. The task completed, the sheep jostle for position to try to get their share of the fodder. Only then is she able to observe the scene, and is devastated by the number of small lamb carcases that litter the paddock, little lambs that failed to survive the night. She laboriously picks each one up, destined for the death pit! There are hundreds of little lambs, bleating sorrowfully around the field, either too young or too weak to be able to follow their mums. Tomorrow morning she realises she will have to pick many of those up as well.

Three ewes are down, and one had a crow perched on top of it. On closer inspection she is able assist the first ewe to its feet, and she waddles off with an unsteady gait. The second ewe has some eye damage inflicted by a crow. She dresses it with a solution she carries in the ute, and this one also is able to rejoin the flock. But the last ewe has lost an eye to the crows. She pours the solution on the eye, and loads the ewe and newly born lamb onto the ute. Neither of them will survive in the paddock, but maybe they will have a slim chance of survival in the shed.

She busies herself during the day mending fences and feeding stock and attending to general farm maintenance work around the property, but always with an eye hopefully on the sky, hoping against hope to see clouds slowly building up! But alas – it's not to be!

She needs to fit into her busy schedule a quick trip to town. They desperately need a supply of groceries. So back home and a quick shower and a change of clothes and off to town, then back home again and another change of clothes and back into the paddocks again!

The monotonous cawing of countless number of crows, scavenging from the small carcases of lifeless lambs, and even attempting to pull live lambs down, make for a heart rending scene

Just prior to sunset she commences her final reconnoitre for the day of the dams. The cow she'd pulled out that morning had not moved.

She knew it never would. With a heavy heart she pulls a rifle from the ute, and pushes a shell into the chamber, and cocks it. She aims and mechanically pulls the trigger. She hears the dull thud of the bullet. Tears fill her eyes, but she doesn't need to look, she knows it is dead. She then began to cry softly, but briefly. The cow had contributed too much to end up like that. It produced a calf every year for the past seven years, and in return all it asked was a square feed and enough water to satisfy its thirst. And they had failed her dismally! That's what hurt the most! The cow had depended on them, trusted them, and they'd failed her! It was not the cow's fault!

She arrives home and prepares the evening meal. Her husband arrives soon after, and in a foul mood. Their children, a girl and a boy, are good kids, but are well aware of the tension, because it is not easy on them either. The boy says something to his sister, and one thing leads to another, and they squabble. It was nothing dramatic, nothing malicious, just sibling bi-play. But their Father explodes, and his reaction is devastating. He ordered both from the table and sent them to their rooms.

Mother and Father are good mates, and support one another all the way. But Mother intervenes this time! She believes passionately in fair play, and by golly, Father is in the wrong! There was no justification in him taking his frustration out on the kids. She feels terribly sorry for him, and knows exactly what he is going through, but the children are not experiencing a bed of roses either. It is very hard on them too! Words are exchanged, and immediately regretted. This was to have been their big year. After twenty years of scrimping and saving to pay off their farm, this was to have been the year they were going to be debt free! They were all going on a holiday. All of them were going to the seaside. The kids have never seen the ocean. They have never been on a holiday – full stop! Their parents have not had a holiday in twenty years. They had all been looking forward to it, but the stinking drought put paid to it! It will take at least another five years to regain lost ground now. And that's if the drought breaks soon! Another five years before they can possibly contemplate planning for a holiday! She can resign herself to accept it. She can dig deep and carry on. But it's so unfair on the kids. She resisted the temptation to shed a tear. There are many generations of country breeding in her genes. She is choc-o-bloc full of grit.

Full of remorse and somewhat chastened by his uncharacteristic outburst, husband retires to bed, dog tired. But sleep does not come easy. The ravages of the drought seem to dominate his thoughts. He fantasises about yarding cattle in knee high pasture. He is approaching the yards, and the calves, with their tails up and curved over their backs, make a break from the herd, and go for a run around the paddock. He is frantically trying to get his dog to round them up, but the little beggars ...are...causi..ng ...mo..re tr..zzzzzz. His wife bends over him "are you okay dear?" He answers "Just let me get these little beggars yarded, an..d..I...zzzzzz. She smiles wryly, and then says a little prayer. Maybe tomorrow will be better, maybe it will rain soon. She settles herself comfortably in bed, and allows her mind to drift unguided over the events of the day.

Oh, because of that kafuffle at the dinner table tonight, she forgot to relate the good news. A little smile played tentatively around her lips. Old Roundup has been transferred. When in town doing the weekly shopping, she met him and he told her the good news. Of course she didn't let on to him it was good news! She had needed to draw funds for the groceries, and as she entered the bank, with much trepidation, as is her custom nowadays, Old Roundup seemed to focus his attention upon her and hurried across. Oh-oh, here comes the crunch, was her immediate reaction, but he actually smiled at her. The very first smile she had seen on his lips in all of five years! Old Roundup was their Bank Manager. He was being transferred somewhere up north, he did say where, but she couldn't remember the place. He actually thanked her for their custom during his period at the helm here, and then went on to say something that literally took the wind out of her sails! It was "I wish all our banks clients were as reliable as you, it certainly makes our job a lot easier". He went on to wish them both the best of luck. She of course responded likewise. She withdrew her money and hurried from the bank, her head held high, and a new found spring in her step. There was a glimmer of light in that long dark tunnel again!

For years they had peered down that long dark tunnel. There were times when the light at the end of it appeared bright and radiant. Other times it appeared so distant and oh so faint. And lately, it seemed to have disappeared completely. But now, there was hope again. You see, the succession of country bank managers appeared to follow a set pattern. She remembers her Father, and her Grandfather both saying the same thing. The banks usually send a good all round guy along as its manager. A real outgoing sort of bloke, one who gets involved in all the communities affairs. His job is to build up the banks clientele base. He is an accumulator, a builder. And this type of manager is usually followed by an Uncle Scrooge type, and his job is to weed out all the credit risks, the dead wood, those high risk patrons. He is basically a weeder, hence the name Old Roundup! Most fatal to unwanted weeds!

So- if the bank is still sympathetic to their cause, then that has got to be a real positive. Of course, there are many hurdles yet to be negotiated, but between them, they will battle on – regardless! Neither of them have been quitters in the past, and are not about to become one now. Not after all the effort they have contributed up to this point in time. She was getting drowsy, and her last legible thought before sleep claimed her was, maybe tomorrow will bring some relief, some rain. Another day – another hope!

Christmas In Hospital

It was a hospital bed - and comfy – but need I say any more?
I was in ward eight, located on the institute's ground floor.
Where the nurses are so kind and their caring very sincere,
But were grossly understaffed cos Christmas time was here!

I'd already spent time recovering in intensive care,
In a private room (but it was boring shut away in there)
I had private insurance but was transferred to a public ward,
And that suited me fine cos now I wouldn't be so bored.

The hospital closed a ward because they lacked the staff,
And apologised to me (then wondered 'bout my laugh!)
But now I had neighbours left and right and one at the foot of my bed,
And we could chat all day – only pausing to be fed!

One evening they admitted a patient when the ambos dropped him off,
And the moment I heard him speak I knew he was a toff.
But my heart grieved cos I twigged he was an Alzheimer,
Cut down in life and deprived of being a cheerful old timer.

And to further complicate his life the poor old chap was blind,
Negating his ability for the shower and toilet to find,
So when the need arose he relied on nurses' help,
And if their response was slow you would hear this pathetic yelp!

"Nurse? Nurse? Where are you nurse? O heck – I've peed myself again!
But the nurses were respectful and did not escalate his pain!
Then some rellies breezed in with an air of educated wealth,
But were more concerned with social status than his bill of health!

"Oh how dreadful Uncle daaarrling what have they done to you?
What are you doing in here among all this motley crew?
Why – you have private insurance – you should be in a private rooooom!"
And her voice echoed 'round the ward like a sonic booooom.

"It's alright Rachel dear these men are very nice,
And I've told them all about my engineering vice".
"No – it's not alright Uncle daaarrling you deserve much more than this,
Where's the Matron? I want words with that manipulating Miss."

She begged and threatened the Matron as she put her Uncle's case,
But the Matron stood firm and fair and not a thing did she retrace.
She made the situation clear and not once did she procrastinate,
"The best care for your Uncle's needs is right here in this ward eight!"

"It's outrageous! Come Uncle daaarrrling – you're coming home with us!
With your community status you don't deserve this fuss!"
So the poor old chap vacated the bed on my right,
And then he and his entourage exited from our sight.

Two days later the wards men wheeled in a patient one evening late,

And the moment he spoke I knew it was our blind Alzheimer mate.
Had his doting niece tired of her dearest Uncle daaarrrling?
Had his social status now declined to that of a common Aussie staaarrrling?

I have no idea what caused his demise (but I'll take a calculated guess)
Alzheimer patients are demanding and can induce family stress.
But it stopped me from worrying about my poor old dodgy ticker,
And realise how fortunate I am (and this healed me even quicker!)

The moral of this story I'm sure lies in human expectation,
Of our status quo – and of our perceived superior education,
But what we often overlook in our quest for public recognition,
Is we are all equal – especially at the point of our attrition!

The Cockies Header

It's time to pull the header out cos harvest is coming fast,
And the weather bureau states this ideal weather will not last.
The crops are maturing and their grain is beginning to harden,
And now's not the time nor place for a stallng exercise,
Cos pound foolish with repairs and a mere penny wise,
Can have consequences for which a farmer does not bargain.

So the header was hauled from the shed hitched to a tractor,
With the pto drive connected (and this is a vital factor)
Then the header was engaged to rid the accumulated residue,
(Just a repeat of what was done when the machine was put in store)
And two rats exited via the riddles along with the dust and chaff and straw.
And the header was ready for the bearing refit the farmer wanted to renew.

Finally the header was pulled into a crop that had grown very tall,
But first the farmer closed the drum cos the grain was very small.
Then he noticed the sample screenings were a little high,
So he lowered the tailboard and increased the riddle blast,
But the riddle became as clean as a whistle (so that didn't last!)
Cos he needed to retain every grain he grew and not eject them nigh.

While rummaging among the tailings he found discarded grain,
And that demanded a settings review (so he changed them all again)

He redirected the blast and opened and lowered the riddles at the rear,
And added more shake and it clicked (as if he were in a dream!)
He didn't lose another grain and his sample was supreme,
So he stripped longer hours cos rain clouds were coming near.

The farmer had an amazing run and reaped the paddock he was in,
And moved into an oaten crop – but first he opened the drum agin,
Then changed the riddle and its blast, and fiddled with the shake,
And removed fingers from the comb to negate a pending choke,
Then all was ready to harvest oats (and all it may invoke)
But the rain clouds kept on gathering – and none of them were fake.

He harvested a range of crops and adjusted his header to suit them all,
Whether they were short or tangled or standing straight and tall,
And not a single minute was lost in replacing a faulty part!
Then following cut out the rains tumbled down – the heavens really bled!
But the header was safely stored away in its protective shed,
Cos the farmer was soundly prepared – and well before the start!

Lost Youth

Two old timers met on the village street,
One was tough and rather uncouth,
The other had poise and was tidy and neat,
And both had been buddies back in their youth.

One began his youth with charm and with flair,
While the other was reserved but full of ambitions,
In maturity one faded and the other became Mayor,
Yet both were mates before their transitions.

"G'day – how are you going mate,
Good to see you up and about again.
I can't say I've seen you 'round of late.
Are you still bothered by those aches and pains?"

"No-no- I'm doin' quite orriite,
Wif sumdays a wee bit bettern others.
Cos I don't git out much now at nite,
But that's a blessin fer all those dotin' mothers."

"Heh-heh, You sure were a Casanova,
When you were young and in your prime.
You must be- what-eighty five? No -over?
Yep- you sure were a dandy in your time."

"I'll have yer know I'll be ninety one tomorry,

*And I've had a pretty darn good sorta life.
Me only regret fer which I'm sorry,
Is I nevva picked me up a wife."*

"It must be pretty crook being on your own,
Without a Missus to share joys and strife,
But what made you choose to live alone?
You had dozens of girls willing to be your wife?"

*"Wal- I thort I was runnin' the poifect race,
I ad em at me mercy round the turn,
But alf way up the strait I kinda lost me pace,
An in no time at all I found meself astern."*

"Mate – they just twigged to your little game,
Carving notches is a game that will not last,
And far and wide you went and spread your fame.
You were just simply overtaken by your past."

*"The shielas about me age all up and chose a mate,
An I couldn't cut the mustard with the youngens left in line.
All of a sudden me luv life started to abate.
An ther I was- sorta free fallen'- and in decline."*

"I sympathise mate but please tell me true,
What was your ultimate goal in life?
You had all of those beautiful girls mad about you,
Yet not one was good enough to be your wife?"

*"Yer wrong mate- thar was one ida had fer sure,
But she reckoned I ad no breedin',
Tol me to op on me bike and don't come round no more,
And then ignored all me beggan and pleaden."*

"Go on? I say- that was a low sort of blow,
Tell me – what sort of girl would thus infer?"
"Wal mate- I reckon by now yuse orta know,
Cos it was yuse who up and married er!"

Ode To Roey

Sale o, sale o. What am I bid for this drover's pup?
Fifty bucks? Fifty is all I ask to get me away.
At fifty bucks it's as cheap as old boots,
And you won't find breeding like this every day.

Come now lads pay attention and give me your bid,
It's where we finish that counts – not where we start,
Well forty bucks? Has anyone got forty to get me away?
Come on fellas loosen up haven't yuh got any heart?

Thirty bucks? Twenty? Okay ten – I'll meet the market,
The auctioneer's call came loud and free,
I proffered one hand with all digits extended,
And the drover's pup was knocked down to me.

She was six weeks old when she came to me,
Jet black with a dash of white on the chest,
Two front white feet and a cheeky tilt to the head,
I knew right then she would rate with the best.

My son wanted to call her Rowena,
A figure of note from Star Wars I'm told,
As a compromise we settled for Roey,
And she bore it with pride til fifteen years old.

She was born to work there's no doubt about that,

And she mastered the craft while still quite young,
She revelled in bending the will of the sheep,
And all dissenters she'd lash with her tongue.

Working cattle was a task she seemed to love best,
And was proud of the respect she got from those moos,
Their reaction was fast whenever she was near,
But she was clearly frustrated by lagging old ewes.

Roey would toil all the morning so full of zest,
Then we'd retire to some shade and share our lunch,
I'd eat my sangers and give her the scraps,
Then I'd throw her the remnants of my apple to munch.

Yeah – we were good mates and our friendship was real,
We'd rest for awhile as we shared the back of our ute,
And if I lingered awhile I'd feel a gentle paw on my hand,
She'd jump down and trot off, and wait my pursuit.

She loved to sit by the 'Bidgee bank where the ripples glided by,
And her keen eyes would spot a stick as it drifted past,
And she would wait til it drifted close to the bank,
Then ringing wet she'd bring back for me to recast.

She'd bark for me to toss it in so she could try again,
But her days were running out 'tho we didn't know it then,
Cos they were carefree days and we were unsuspecting,
We'd forgotten how the devil lurks in the hearts of certain men.

The life of my treasured friend was brutally taken one day,
By the evil hand of a rebel of our very own human race,
One so confined by limits of a miniature world of his own,
Where you and I and canine friends will never find a place!

All the local foxes were the targets of his aggression,
Cos he laid his bates far and wide – even on our selection,
But for the torturous death of my friend,
His dastardly deed would've escaped our detection.

When an offender can snub the laws of our land,
What value is the life of a truly wonderful friend?
When he's told to go on home and don't do it again?
Pardon me – but I'm bitter towards this legalistic trend!

Roey was then fifteen – and fast approaching sixteen,
But still choc-o bloc full of vigour and vim,
 Well – maybe her hearing was becoming impaired,
And yes- her eyesight was slowly growing dim.

Even so she was willing to tackle a full day's work,
And how terribly sad she'd be if I chose to leave her home.
I still fancy I see her, grinning as she surveys from the rear of my ute.
Or relaxing by the "Bidgee, watching the ripples, the leaves, and foam

I don't know if the rebel is sorry, cos he's never bothered to say,
One day I may forgive him, but right now we'll not share a cup,
Because I cherished those wonderful times we shared, my friend,
And I'll never regret the day I purchased you – as a drover's pup!

Cricket Trials

I was padded up and I had my trusty bat in hand,
As I strode towards the concrete matted wicket,
I was determined to stay and make a stand,
Despite it being my first game in senior cricket.

It was the beginning of the new season trials,
To find new talent (if any were around)
And some travelled in from many miles,
Just to watch or trial at the local cricket ground.

I recalled advice as I nervously took my stance,
(To keep my bat straight and eyes glued upon the ball)
But I resolved to go the slog if ere I got the chance,
Cos as a tailender – why hang around and stonewall?

The first ball I cover drove to the fence,
And we scrambled through for three,
Then my partner hit a single (and meaning no offence)
The last ball of the over was now left up to me.

The bowl drifted to leg and I hooked it hard for four,
(Now bear in mind I was batting at number eleven)
Next ball my partner was out – and cos we had no more,
I carried my bat with a score of not out seven.

It wasn't great but I thought I'd be in contention,

Cos my potential was in my off breaks when I bowled,
But I spent the match in the outfield (now that wasn't my intention)
And my bowling talent remained permanently on hold.

They said I had some talent (I caught three and ran one out!)
But there'd be no vacancies in their team again this year.
I was urged to come again cos they felt there was no doubt,
They liked my style and the potential there was clear.

So I joined the local tennis club to while away my time,
And I grew to love the sport and their member's style,
Now I'm not sure if this constitutes a reason or a rhyme,
But the fact is, I never did attend another cricket trial!

People In The Mall

Me an me mate were discussing politicians,
Where the air conditions,
At a local shopping mall,
And while we were talking,
I was kind of gawking,
At the ladies strutting past our stall,
They were all shapes and sizes,
And some would never win no prizes,
And others so lovely they took me breath an all!

Now me an me mate are pretty good talkers,
And some of those sheilas were top notch corkers,
Well – as good as you're ever likely to see.
But can you tell me 'bout the garments,
Worn by some of those young varmints,
Is there a fabric shortage in the clothing industry?
Me an me mate – well we agree,
That is, as far as we can see,
Their epidermis exposure would rival the fruit on any tree.

Now me an me mate are a bit long in the tooth,
 So we judge strictly on the hoof,
And we're uneasy 'bout this unveiling of the skin.
We know they are a new generation,
Deleting the need for imagination,
But what about the effects on obesity and the thin?
Now me an me mate are cattle breeders retired,
And selected our herds by appraisals truly tried,
And we reckon there's an urgent need to cull right here within.

Me an me mate – now we enjoy our share of fun,

And all the freedom that we've won,
From working on our farms – and at risk of sounding uncouth,
We sit and leisurely peruse,
The ultimate under use,
Of the fabric, in the scanty apparel being worn by our youth!
So let's explore the actualities,
For any possible practicalities,
By getting down to tin tacks an exposing the naked truth!

Me an me mate – well we was kind of wondering,
When those winter frosts come a plundering,
Wouldn't they suffer from frost bite 'round the belly?
And with their necklines dropping,
And showing no signs of stopping,
The scorching sun must surely give 'em helly!
And those mini shirts,
With their mini skirts,
On a freezing winters day? No - not on your flipping Nellie!

Me an me mate are quite confused,
And more than a little amused,
By the surplus flesh crammed into a skimpy little ensemble.
If they bend over – ahem!
But if they squat down –amen!
These fashion styles are simply not for our truly humble.
But there are a few of mature age,
Who think this style is all the rage,
And dress accordingly in a last ditch effort to rumble.

While me an me mate ensure we are positioned,
In the Mall, and settle where the air's conditioned
We wonder if this mode of dress is really practical
We reckon it is probably a style,
That some will wear for awhile,
Before their stratagem becomes a little more tactical!
Now me an me mate try to be fair,
And agree – apart from a little flair,
These skimpy fashions are, quite simply, impractical!

The Cowabbie Cup

The day dawned grey and windy,
For the annual Cowabbie Cup,
And the sky was threatening and spewy,
Like the day could easily erupt!

Now there was a horse called Mukkatah,
A big upstanding grey,
That created a little interest,
When paraded on the day.

But all the money was on the flashy black,
From down old Grong Grong way,
Cos he's reported to be a faster horse,
Then the Walsh's upstanding grey.

The grey is off their Newlyn's run,
And is as honest as the day is long,
And when they near the finish line,
He'll still be running on strong.

Four other horses are in the race,
But none are favoured this day,
Cos none of them can hold a candle,
To the flashy Black or Grey!

The flashy black is a flighty type,
And his breeding clearly shows,
And upon his back for just this race,

He'll have one of the leading pros.

The rangy grey is a cockies nag,
He's relaxed and kind of docile,
But when the occasion so demands,
You can count on a speedy mile.

With a butt of clover seed up on the saddle
Mukkatah walked the sown fields,
While seed was dispersed beside each flank,
To help soil fertility and future yields.

But he's content and more at home,
When droving a mob of sheep,
Whereas the flashy black is bred to race,
And that breeding runs so deep.

The Marshall's call rang loud and clear,
"It's time to saddle yer 'orses",
An though it gets the same result,
It's not heard it on metropolitan courses.

Suddenly the threatening sky erupted,
And the rain just pelted down
Till the track was quickly sodden,
And declared to be out of bound!

They were forced to postpone the cup,
And reschedule for another day,
For the flashy black from Grongy,
To challenge the big rangy grey!

It was an anti climax in a way,
With expectations well below par,

Cos many had wagered the flashy black,
But there was support for Mukkata.

The flashy black returned again,
For the rescheduled Cowabbie Cup,
Plus there was a smoky from Ardlethan,
That raised many an eyebrow up.

And the big rangy grey from Newlyn's,
Returned to claim his spot,
As well as three or four others,
Tho the day was steaming hot.

Now this was wonderful for the ladies,
In their gaily printed frocks,
But a feature was their headdress,
Creating many domestic shocks

In all seven runners were in the race,
And the starter – with a nervous cough,
Dropped his flag and they jumped as one,
And the crowd all shouted "They're off".

Now it was the flashy black from Grongy,
Who showed the way early in the race,
But that smoky from Ardlethan,
Was matching him for pace!

But the rangy grey from Newlyn's,
With the young O'Reilly up,
Tailed the field and was at the rear,
In his first Cowabbie Cup,

Around the bend as they headed for home,

Came the smoky and flashy black,
Matched neck and neck and stride for stride,
As they thundered down the track,

One was sure to be first to the post,
Less than two hundred metres away,
When suddenly up went an excited shout,
"Look! Here comes that rangy grey

They had no idea how he'd got so close,
Cos he was never in contention,
Their eyes had been glued to the smoky and black,
But now it was Mukkata with all their attention.

He closed the gap in two or three strides,
With young 'Reilly wielding the old gee-up,
Then another stride and his nose was in front,
And Mukkata won the cup!

The crowd erupted as only bush crowds do,
When their local wins on the day,
And they all joined in one huge ovation,
For the big upstanding grey!

Back on the farm and all the excitement gone,
And the grey at his oaten lunch,
You wondered how one so meek and mild,
Could down such a classy bunch!

Well – each day he continually trailed the sheep,
So why trail his peers all day?
I guess frustration proved too much,
 For the Walsh's upstanding grey.

Harry's Son

Billy was the Postmaster,
Down old Grong Grong way,
And Harry was the Stationmaster,
After both agreed to stay.
And I was just the night boy – at the Grongy 'phone exchange,
Where I answered all the night calls – that were 'phoned in off our range

Now Harry had a wife,
And she was now expecting,
It was their decision late in life,
And they needed our protecting.
But I was just the night boy – at the Grongy phone exchange,
And my job was to answer the night calls – that were phoned in off our range.

Now Harry had no blower,
Connected to his abode,
So memos reached him slower,
And his calm would often erode.
Now I was just the night boy – at the Grongy phone exchange,
And I couldn't ring old Harry – cos he wasn't on our range

Then Billy and Harry cooked this idea up instead,
(And I'll repeat here for what it's worth!)
When Harry's wife is finally laid abed,

The Sister could phone and alert me of the birth!
But I am just the night boy – at the Grongy phone exchange,
And I can't ignore those night calls – and go out and leave the range!

But Billy assured me all would be okay,
Just turn the alarm on full and off you go,
And should a call come in while you're away,
Why I'll get up and run the jolly show!
Now I was just the night boy – at the Grongy phone exchange,
And here I am waiting for Harry's night call – Cos Harry's off our range.

Three am I get the call and I leave with no desire to tarry,
And nearing his home I hear his voice call oh so wan,
So I responded with "Congratulations Harry,
You have just got yourself a son".
And I was just the night boy – at the Grongy phone exchange,
And here I am at old Harry's – cos Harry isn't on our range.

Back at the switchboard I settled down again,
Determined to get some shuteye,
But that walk had sort of cleared my brain,
And I cannot sleep no matter how I try.
For I was just the night boy – at the Grongy phone exchange,
And I'd walked my way to Harry's – cos he wasn't on our range.

Now Artie is a station boss,
In charge of the great Western Run,
And he decides if you sleep or toss,
And even when your day begun!
Cos I was just the night boy – at the Grongy phone exchange,
And Artie begins ringing at four thirty – and he's the big wig on our range!

Doc Harry

They wheeled me into the operating theatre,
And Doc Harry greeted with his usual beaming smile.
His stubby whiskers were still prolifically growing,
In a vigorous agricultural kind of style

I'd been admitted for a procedure known as TURP,
Or to be precise a trans urethral resection of the prostrate,
After Doc Harry agreed to take this liberating course,
And all I had to do was relax, submit, and cooperate.

The anaesthetist was also waiting there,
And as I had previously been told,
He pricked me with a needle in the spine,
And the whole procedure then began to unfold.

They'd draped me in a ridiculous sort of gown,
And there I lay, humiliated – but composed,
Til Doc Harry pulled the flimsy garment back,
And there I was, completely all exposed!

But the mixed company were all professionals,
And nudity was no concern, cos I was a presenter,
Of interesting little nooks and orifices,
Through which they often used to enter.

By now my legs were devoid of any feeling,

And my rump so heavy it may have been cast in stone,
So I settled down to watch the tiny TV screen,
But things became so foggy and I felt so all alone.

I've no idea what happened next til I became aware,
I was being wheeled again – back into my room,
All seemed well and all were acting casual,
With no hint of any pending gloom.

Back in my room I then assessed the situation.
I had a drip at the top and one at the foot of my bed,
(We'll ignore the one prostrate in the middle!)
All I could move were my hands and my head.

"Now see if you can wriggle your toes darling",
Urged the nurse (the one with a facial wrinkle)
And I did all I could in an effort to comply,
But I couldn't even raise a simple tiny twinkle.

The drip up front was connected to my hand,
So with the other I decided to explore,
And discovered a catheter attached to His Nibs,
With a long tube running right down to the floor!

I was acutely aware of my immobility,
Now if for reasons we had to evacuate,
And me with legs that would not even function,
And a stoned bum (is there need further elucidate?)

After six hours I felt a sensation down in my toes,
And I could move them, but only by rolling my legs as well!
But small as the movements were it was really such a relief,
Cos soon I would be spending less of my time in hell!

So I settled down for the night in the bowels of AWPH,
The nurses were tremendous and cared for my needs and more.
And with monitoring drips and exchanging bags of waste,
They were constantly in and out my door.

The morning's ablutions were scary amid the trolleys and the drips,
But old Doc Harry arrived right on the eleventh hour,
And said "Strip off all that irrigation stuff and get it right away,
And let the man enjoy an unencumbered shower".

Later the tube had to be reattached to the catheter,
And the catheter was already attached to me!
It was humiliating - but was the shower worth it?
Tho the nurses were great, it tested my humility!

Later that day the sister suggested I stroll out in the hall.
"What? With His Nibs adorned in brilliant array,
With catheter and tubes and a bag half full of wee?"
"Okay – you just sit and relax and have a lovely day".

Early next morning before the sun could rise,
'Twas time for the catheter to go cos no longer required,
And a male nurse with confidence and professional aplomb,
Explained so clearly the teamwork he desired

"Now put your hands on your chest and take deeply breath,
And slowly exhale – now repeat"- and my catheter was out!
It was a relief to be free of the tubes and that encumbering bag,
And be whole again! And in charge of my spout!

Prostrate is not a dirty word – it's a common part of us,
Treat it as you would your car – give it regular service,
Cos like a car things go wrong and mal-function,
But don't worry, there's no need to be nervous!

I now have the power to hit a sparrow,
At five paces (it's just my aim I need to adjust!)
So if you are facing a similar fate – take heart,
 Doc Harry's the man for you – and one you can truly trust!

The Class Of Forty Three

Can you fast track your memory without fear of disparity,
And take it back a decade - or maybe two or three,
And then recall events that happened with complete clarity,
And renew cherished friendships with passion and ecstasy?

Well I know an intriguing mob who can do exactly that,
In fact they can go all the way back to nineteen forty three,
The year they sat their intermediate (now a bit of old hat)
Before they invaded an unsuspecting world – all original and free!

They lived their early maturing lives in the shadow of the lion,
Either residing in or around the village of The Rock,
And in a corporate search for data their spirits did entwine,
And of course it's not unusual for those spirits to interlock.

In time unbridled talent emerged from within those genial ranks,
As there were several top stenographers well versed in the ABC,
And a couple of leading farmers and one who managed banks,
And all of them were produced from that class of forty three.

Another became a teacher and excelled at all within her range,
While two others reached the pinnacle in private enterprise,
And a couple became telephonists and ruled the phone exchange,
While several married farmers which will come as no surprise

Now others established careers within the essential services,

And rose to be high in the ranks like that of the PMG,
Several others chose the railway – and all it encompasses,
And all of them were the products of that class of forty three.

They meet together every year or so just to chew the fat,
And to recall events that happened so many years ago,
Now some of the yarns they tell can really raise your hat,
Yet they've never had a tendency to allow any of them to grow!

Four of those lads kept pigeons (which isn't a crime of course)
But they captured them where neither bird nor boy could see!
At night – high atop a wheat silo (mind you it was their only source)
But I reckon death may have flirted with that class of forty three!

They talk about the time they found a brand new swimming pool,
With panoramic views the like they'd never seen before,
Where the water was so crystal clear and oh so cool,
But what a shame it was the water supply in the village reservoir!

They dived and splashed and swam all through the arvo long,
And cleaned away the mud and grime after their dip in a nearby creek.
It was after they told their Mums they grasped it was all wrong,
Then suddenly the subject was closed and no one dared to speak!

They are a happy congenial bunch which nobody can deny,
But just how serious did they view their sums and their ABC?
Did they give their teachers what-oh or were they as nice as pie?
Cos I know there are some 'rascals' in that class of forty three!

Some of the class moved over the border to reside in a foreign land,
While most of them are true blue and stayed in New South Wales,
But states are not a barrier to liaisons of this very special brand,
As is witnessed by the fervour they pursue them over hills and dales.

You cannot tell of this special group without mention of leader Bob,
He hails from south of the border and I say that respectfully,
Cos he has become their guiding light as he gently steers the mob,
Yes – it is he who inspires this ageless class of nineteen forty three!

Their ranks remain basically intact but are missing several spouses,
And they will continue to gather for as long as the Lord reprieves,
Cos inspiration is their reward from the contacts their emotion arouses,
And this highlights the influence of friendships – and what it all achieves.

Maybe you are wondering why it is I hold them all in awe,
Or how I know them all so well when I hail from another locality?
Well the answer is really simple and I should have said before,
I married one of those gems from that class of forty three!

Our Awesome Lord

I am just a humble farmer but I see a lot of God.
(I mean – testimonies of his presence are here for all to see)
If we would only take the time to impartially survey,
All the wonders this universe presents to you and me.

Have you ever had the urge to eject from your bed at dawn,
And revel in exposure to a late autumn morn?
Have you ever been in awe of the hue of the gently falling leaves,
And the splendour of the trees which those leaves adorn?

Have you listened to melodious birds as they shrug off the cloak of night,
And preen their gaily coloured feathers and greet the rising sun?
Is all this beauty lost upon you, or are you really wise,
And know and are in awe of all our Lord has done?

Have you exited from your bed on a cold and frosty morn,
And marvelled at the snow white crust upon your shrubs and lawn?
Then watched the brilliant rays of sun with all its warmth and soul,
Restore colour and life to where that frost was worn?

Have you ever rugged up tight against the falling rain,
Or loitered in a garden where the leaves glistened with morning dew,
Or bathed in the golden sun free from winters chills,
Or sat alone at sunset and admired its brilliant hue?

Have you had an urge to leap from bed before the day's begun,
And strolled on a bright spring morn watching the rising sun,
And viewed the array of brilliant flowers and the fullness of bursting buds?
And not been inspired or awed by what our Lord has done?

Have you shared the thrill of watching the birth of a lamb,
And been beguiled as the mother kindles its spirit from within,
And then been enthralled as the lambs rises on quivering legs,
Then turns to Mum for the foster it knows there is therein?

All this happens in the time it takes to enjoy your morning tea,
And if our Lord is not involved how can it possibly be,
For the knowledge to exist with one so young to know just what to do,
Surely the powers of our awesome Lord are there for all to see?

Parched fields and searing heat and the water is running low,
While sheep and cattle circle the dam with barely a week to go,
Before the water will be gone and the farmer mops his brow,
And with laboured steps turns towards a future so full of woe.

Only a heavy soaking rain can save the day and turn the scene around,
And heavy clouds gather on the horizon as the dawn heralds the day.
A butcher bird leads and the magpies chorus in a catchy lyrical tune,
While the farmer kneels and bows his head and silently begins to pray.

Late that night he spills from his bed at some unearthly hour,
Cos he was noisily awakened from his slumber by a heavily falling shower,
The thunder roars and the lightning strikes and pierces the summer night,

And the farmer silently worships his Lord and all of his awesome power.

Gifts And Talents

I went along this morning to our local church,
And attended a "Sing our Faith" type of service,
All the Hymns we sang were chosen by research,
By Nancy (who now appeared quite nervous!)

I settled myself down there in my pew,
Thinking of the chores back home I have do,
And I think the next item was given a mention,
In the announcements – but escaped my attention!

Until this sweetest melody gently caressed my ears,
So I leaned back in my seat completely now enthralled,
Cos it was the loveliest sound I heard in many years,
And if any sweeter I think I could have balled!

This melody was sung by two males as a duet,
And you'll hear no better on the internet!
Yet they are just a pair of humble guys,
Who like you and I have had their lows and highs.

Now each of them is blessed with a very special gift,
And sing with pride about their faith and praise,
And inspire others as they give a very special lift,
With their talents that never cease to amaze.

Everyone has been gifted with a voice,

('Tho perhaps not one of our own choice)
So do not envy others and allow ours to stop and stall,
But spare a thought for those who cannot speak at all!

Thomas was gifted with loads of human compassion,
'Tho he struggled to impart with self expression!
But he exuded talent in an uniquely Thomas fashion,
And never wallowed in the depths of self depression!

All of us are given talents for a very special reason,
And for a time and place – there'll always a season!
So let's accept and own them – and let us daily use,
Cos only soon enough– those gifts we will lose!

Lord, We Heard You Calling!

I awakened suddenly, and while waiting for my sanity to arrive,
I was wondering where the heck I was, and if I was still alive!
But then as reality struck, and I became conscious of the time,
A quarter to five? Now the next fifteen minutes will be sublime!

I used it all to plan my day, before clamouring from my bed,
And I stumbled to the kitchen fridge, determined to be fed.
You see, I am a mission co-ordinator, or whatever that may mean,
And I help to organise outreach programmes, and all in between.

It's an inspiring occupation and it helps to keep one off the street,
And there's an intriguing group of people always waiting for you to meet,
But organising helpers is a treat that you will always have in store,
Because this bunch of loyal volunteers you just simply can't ignore.

And if you tend little children by serving breakfast in their schools,
There are regulations, and you must pay strict attention to the rules,
Some are cute little mites and you'll often crave to hug those souls,
But if you disregard protocol, then you will not be kicking any goals!

As a caring church we heard the call and prepared ourselves to embrace,
Our Food Ministry, and we nurtured it until it could proudly take its place,

As an icon of our community with a clientele continually growing fast,
And it distributes provisions twice weekly and those quantities are vast.

If you go next door to the Drop-In you will meet some wonderful folks,
Although you may assess one or two as being strange sorts of blokes,
And it's an education because you'll see how some are forced to live,
As well as an insight into your own soul and what it's prepared to give!

If you crave for an outing that has excitement and loads of fellowship,
We run a Friday Night Fiesta that'll render this, as well as comradeship,
And a three course meal at a nominal cost and loads of entertainment too,
It's a night you will well remember and your desire for fiestas will accrue.

Christmas is a joyous time when we can get to celebrate our Lord's birth,
But for so many it can be sad time, completely bereft of humour and of mirth,
Perhaps a dear one has suddenly passed away and left an elderly spouse alone,
Or maybe a lone parent lacks the resources, and with a family not yet grown.

We heard this call for a Christmas mission, and we decided to take all in hand,

And we've created Christmas lunches ever since in response to this demand,
And we have an amazing rapport with all the volunteers from our community,
And we all support each other in true Christmas faith, as we work in unity.

It's a great feeling when you can offer this assistance wherever it is needed,
Especially to the less fortunate when all their hope seems to have receded
But it is sad when you realise these programmes have really become essential,
And when comparing effort versus rewards, then effort becomes inconsequential!

All Aboard For Twenty Twenty

We were all gathered at the station, waiting for further information,
When the guard called "Next train leaves in five minutes for Twenty Twenty",
Our mood then became more urgent and we began acting like an insurgent,
As we clamoured frantically to find a seat, and avoid being named as absentee

Now what can we really expect, barring great fortune or sheer neglect,
Will Twenty Twenty be the challenge for us to display some of our compassion?
Can we really change our ways and show concern in the coming days,
Or will we continue to live out our lives, in an uncompromising fashion?

We'll submit a New Year resolution that'll lead to our future evolution,
But being fully aware it'll take lots of courage and determination to fulfil,
Because it only takes a simple contraction, to create an entire abstraction,
And all our best efforts to achieve will just simply amount to nil.

We'll need to get our priorities right and pray for their success every night
And if granted by our Lord it'll be subject to His will and variation,
So we need to seriously observe and be ever ready to subserve
Because if and when our loving Lord calls us, it will be by invitation

So is it possible that Twenty Twenty can become the year of plenty,
Or will it continue as an unrelenting drought, creating sadness unabated?
Will fires continue to torment the earth denying many families of their mirth,
Or will it be a different scenario, comprised of something unrelated?

Can we become a loving church community, endorsing harmony and unity?
Or in Twenty are we destined to become two opposing factions?
Our Executive is a class act, and fiddling with Council fabric will further detract
So let's proceed with governing our church, with only positive actions.

We're a church group with an unclear expectation, as our train leaves the station,
And we are worrying what Twenty has in store for us and how on earth we'll cope,
Well now's the time to consult our Lord and invite Him here to come on board
And His will to become our basis for all discussions, thus presenting us with hope

Enforced Isolation

Yeah, I was pretty irate when told it was time for me to vacate,
The Ministry I'd founded and ran for fifteen years,
Yes I am over seventy five but I felt I'd been relegated to the archive,
And unceremoniously demoted, as it appears,
But what I found hard to overcome was the lack of feedback there from some,
And I'm still completely left here in the dark,
However, whatever word I did receive, I could only construe was to deceive,
So I'm resting faithfully and waiting to re-embark.

What are you doing to the Ministry? Is it going to be the end of this much needed dynasty?
Were just some of the queries I had need to allay,
So is this going to be the end of your reign? Or will you get involved in something once again?
Are often calls that I receive almost every day,

And I received some dire predictions regarding our Ministry's future convictions,
While here in isolation in my home,
But I'd made it very plain from the start, while in isolation I'd be playing no further part
And whatever comes is bound to come.

Now while lingering here in isolation, I had the time to consider any future eventuation,
And to consider what lies ahead of us in store,
I'm thankful for God's early intervention, that may well minimise the risk or even the prevention,
Of the chance of contracting that dreaded virus core

Because while I was the leader there in charge, I was fully exposed and totally at large,
To a virus carrier, should one venture through our door,
But being an aged volunteer in isolation, I am now spared the threat of such a violation,
And while resting here at home, those threats I'm able to ignore,

I've heard various claims about Ministers of the Word, and many of them have often been absurd,
But the lady at Wesley loves to go the extra mile (and far beyond!)
And she has a super duper spouse, but neither of them get to frequently visit their own house,
 They are so dedicated and committed they need a magic wand.

Together they've created a fantastic Scottish team, for which other parishes often pray and dream
Because their priority is to lead their congregation well,
Each Sunday Service is meticulously prepared, and delivering it is a task they both have shared,
But running the Food Ministry is where they both excel.

My enforced isolation has been really good, it's rekindled a love for gardening I didn't think it would,
And now our garden is destined to be the winner,
I have undertaken strenuous work, like tasks I was previously only too willing to shirk,
And now, I'm as fit as a Mallee Bull, but albeit a little thinner.

Yes, I had ample time to sit there pondering, but also was often left there wondering,
Just what is the message God is attempting to relay?
There are Bible quotes that clearly state, if God is for us, then just who else or what can relate?
If we need further clarification then for it we must pray!

Not once do I miss those early morning rises or any of those daily unscheduled surprises,
Even though they created the basics for our days,
Although I do miss the contact with our client because it's on us they'd all become reliant,
And their responses were so rewarding in many ways,

Are our lives destined to change direction? Do we consult with God before making a final selection?
Because it is not wise to go it alone and freelance,
Everyone needs the support of divine power, and God is always available every single hour,
And if we accept Him, we'll be thrilled how our lives enhance.

But in any case we all need to play our small part, and following Jesus is a very good start,
As we wait to see what our future will involve.
But we'll need to show more compassion, and not ignore it as though it's gone from fashion,
Because it's not around us the future will revolve

The Country Lamb Market In The Fifties

Grong Grong sponsored a fat lamb sale, every fortnight without fail,
For the local and neighbouring vendors to market their annual draft,
Where the buyers would bid and clamour as the lambs went under the hammer,
And the tension often rose as these pro buyers demonstrated their craft.

They're pros through and through and knew the values they'd have to pursue,
As they went about amassing the large quota of lambs they usually had to meet.
If they fail to purchase they lose commission, but earning a living's also part of their mission,
So it becomes a fine line between employer and self, with a need to keep their integrity complete.

A large percentage of purchases from the sale were trucked out on the locomotive rail,
And the Grong Grong sales complex was adjacent to the railway trucking yards,
So when the sale was finally over the auctioneer and the yards men all became a drover,
When the consignments for their various clients were carefully despatched with their regards

We discard old practises to give way to future growth (But wouldn't it be nice to share a bit of both?)
But whatever the enterprise and in whatever form it takes, progress should never be denied
While discreet rumblings were beginning to arise regarding the viability of this local enterprise,
The lure of city sales was eroding its client base, on which the local market desperately relied.

Paddock sales direct to an abattoir and Super Market contracts were slowly closing the door,
And better roads and larger, more sophisticated transport, all encouraged the markets demise,
Although the writing was clearly on the wall, they gallantly held on for as long as they could stall,
Before sadly closing down this much loved and rewarding, long established country enterprise.

A huge loss, and a blow to unity, they'd fostered respect among the urban and rural community,
Cos every second Tuesday was in focus, when catering staff prepared the midday meal with pride,
At midday they'd sit to roasts and salads and eagerly gormandise, and then find time to socialize,
But with the markets closure, every aspect of it existence is gone, merely drifted by the way-side.

Progress is great, but can also be a horrible word, because some of its residue is often quite absurd,
And it is doubtful if the resulting consequences are researched and scientifically valuated,
It'd be great for a component from yesteryear to merge with changes we're now becoming to fear,

It could save a lot of heart ache and pave the way for progress to become smoothly integrated.

The Lamb Market helped hold together a community, now that town's lost a chunk of its immunity,
To self disintegration, through lack of community pride in its public achievements and participation,
We had no wish to render its future catastrophic, as we allowed our evolutions to turn philosophic,
As due to good roads we took our trade to larger towns and cities, encouraging further degeneration

And I'll Think To Myself, What A Wonderful Day

This Covid 19 pandemic has sent alarming panic throughout the depths of our whole nation,
Creating inconvenience as we have seen many of our liberties shut down, all to our dismay,
And while the elderly have been confined to their homes, with little there to create elation,
Yet when reviewing events prior to bed, many may think to themselves "I've really enjoyed today".

Now while tucked away in isolation one can become bored, but it is really up to you,
Just keep in mind all the rules and regulations we're obliged to remember and obey,
You may decide to clean the cupboards you've avoided for so long, and you commence without ado,
And just before you retire at night, you quietly think to yourself, "I've had a great rewarding day".

You need to put on hold all your past habits, and get yourself involved in a completely new program,
To pass the time I took up gardening, and communicating with nature in a very meaningful way,
And I'm enjoying it, but one needs to have a blueprint, and stick to every facet of the diagram,

At the end of the day you'll look back with pride, and think to yourself, "I've had a wonderful day".

When gardening out front I've noticed pedestrians who for years have scurried past our gate,
With a mobile phone in hand, plugged up ears with no indication there is anything they want to say,
Well they still stroll by, but now will pause to have a chat, and query, "What are you planting mate?"
And when I finish and retire at night, my face all aglow, I think to myself "I've had a terrific day".

When I was young I lived in a small country town, where everyone was known to one another,
And when we met we'd pause for chat, and whatever news we had we were willing to convey,
Now today that's a blast from the past, emphasising a craving we still like to chat with each other
So spread around some good days with lots of smiles then marvel, at how it brightens up your day,

You only need secateurs or gardening fork in hand, to entice pedestrians to pause and have a talk,
And they can become a wealth of knowledge with all their short cuts and varied cultivating ways,
But their ways of organizing a garden will differ, and we can become alike as cheese and chalk,
But it's great to compare diverse ideas, and be grateful they were willing to contribute to our days.

Maybe you miss going out and mingling with your friends, and joining in those weekly rendezvous,
Or you'll crave for those lazy Sunday lunches, with your favourite group down there at the RSL cafe,

We all endure the same sanctions, but eagerly wait to hear "Now begin to do whatever you choose"
And when we sit to dine again, I'm going to smile and think to myself, "Oh, it IS a wonderful day"!

Covid 19 is lethal and a devastating disease, and its pillaging throughout the world is catastrophic,
 Recovery will take years and there'll be enforced changes as we surge forward in any future forays,
Now some customs and enterprises may bite the dust, if circumstances render them uneconomic,
But despite all the gloom and doom, we retain the power to create some really wonderful days

My Emmaus Walk

I began my Emmaus Walk one cold July weekend,
And it was a stroll I can thoroughly recommend.
Cos the way those men all openly honoured God,
Clearly demonstrated He is their Staff and Rod

And the fellowship always there on offer,
Exceeded what other ado's seldom seem to proffer.
So should you receive an invite, do not hesitate to go,
Cos your faith will be enriched, and it may even grow.

And the early morning worship seemed so sacred and sublime,
(Despite the early start at such a serious choice of time!)
Then we'd file out for our breakfast, singing the words of De Colores,
And we sensed the presence of God, right there before us!

Now the singing thru this Walk was so great to behold,
It was like God reaching out with His arms to enfold!
And the testimonies of those sincerest men of God,
Were highlights of this Walk, as down His path we trod.

Then on the Saturday night, right at the fall of dark,
We boarded a bus, without knowing where it was due to park,
But it parked beside a darkened church that seemed so deserted,
(Which could have been a threat had we been unconverted!)

Those out of the loop assumed we'd been brought along to pray,
But then we received an agape that blew us all away!
Add to that the closing Sunday service,
Then you'll know why we were emotional and nervous!

I've heard of men walking miles just to seek out treasure,
And there are many more who walk, simply for the pleasure.
And even hunters walk miles in search of prey to stalk,
But there's nothing to compare – with <u>my</u> Emmaus Walk.

Wen Oi Wos Yung

Struth! It only seems like yesterdy – an all,
When oi was doin the Barn Dance in thuh old Grongy hall!
And yet oi kin recall every single word oi sed,
Tho it was years ago, theys jus keeps runnin thru me ead.
Oi recall dancin wif me neighbour then biddin er adieu,
Then turnin round an seein this vision dressed in blue.
She looked bloomin gorgeous and softly called "Hello Phil",
Blimey! Oi member mutterin sumpthin afor feelin like a dill!
Oi'd only knowed er all me life and yet, still said sumpthin stupid!
Wot oi really needed then was a 'elpin and' from Cupid!

Life can be a gamble I have heard so many people say,
And it can take many turns as you journey on your way.
But if you play your cards right and are aware of all the bumps,
There's no reason in the world why you cannot come up trumps!

We both lived inna same district and oi ad the ots for er,
(Or, oi thort she was a corker – if thats wot yude prefer)
Now oi'd luvved to av gone an arsk er fer a date,
But oi was sure as eggs she'd say no, an me gall wood then abate!
Oi'd tried tuh psyche meself and convince me oi wus wrong,
But then when face to face me art wood sing anuvver song!
She started daten a weirdo – a real proper billy goat,
And when they got engaged, wal, then oi knowed oi'd missed the boat.
But when she up and wed im oi got as mad as ell,

Cos oi knowed oi ad a chance, but, jus didn't andle it real well!

Your journey thru life can be difficult but its course is up to you.
It can be full of happiness or sadness it depends on what you do.
Some people wind up filthy rich and others very poor,
But you win either way, if you're happy, and stay within the law.

Now all over where sheep graze on clover,
Jus no wun gives a fig fer a arf arted luvver.
Oi knowed oi adtuh update an git me libido intuh gear,
But first oi'd haftuh rid meself ov all this senseless fear.
Cupid were me role model so oi carefully studied thuh bloke,
    But doin all thuh stuff e did shorely were no joke!
But oi worked ard til oi poifected the poifect plan,
Tuh make me as amorous as any uvver man.
But wen the rite wun cum along it mocked the plans of men,
Fer we knowed jus wot ter say, cos it all cum nactherly then!

To evaluate your life it's not about reaching all your goals,
It's about humility, and reaching out to other souls.
You may be the most brilliant person here on earth,
But devoid of humility, your past will not record your worth!

Volunteers

"There are volunteers, and there are volunteers",
The man on the soap-box said.
"Although many have peers, few are peerless,
It's all about the mind-set in their head".

A co-ordinator's dream is a dedicated volunteer,
One whose mind-set and heart are so sincere
They don't come for personal gain or just to feel good,
They come out of concern for their brother and sisterhood.

"A Clayton's volunteer is a useless volunteer",
And the man on the soapbox said so.
"The day before they'll be looking for offers,
Then apologise cos they 'have' to go".

A co-ordinator's curse is a 'Clayton's' volunteer,
One with a willing mind-set but whose heart is insincere.
They're rostered but leave their door ajar for better propositions
And when they come are not deterred by last minute transitions.

"A volunteer with an ego is a volunteer to let go",
The man on the soap-box once inferred.
"Cos in volunteering the next step is domineering,
'Despatch quickly' is the process best preferred".

A co-ordinator's nightmare is a know-all volunteer,

Who want to change the system the moment they appear.
The plight of the charity is the furthest from their heart,
And if their mind-set concurs they're trouble from the start.

"What's your version of a selfish volunteer?"
The man on the soap-box coyly asks.
"Someone who always seeks advantage,
'What's in it for me when I do these tasks'?"

A co-ordinator's problem is a selfish volunteer,
(And I'll defy you to define exactly why they're here!)
They assume the role of shepherd but really are lost sheep,
Cos once the fields have ripened, they're the first ones in to reap!

"Tell me – what is a compassionate volunteer?"
The man on the soap-box was heard to inquire.
"One who empathises with those they serve,
Who will listen, encourage and endeavour to inspire.

It's what a co-ordinator dreams of – a compassionate volunteer,
And I believe all our workers are up there on that tier.
They quietly do the task God has called them for,
And they do it with love, and never regard it as a chore.

Grong Grong Sheep Sale

George was selling a pen of young merino ewes,
"Two tooth hoggets-just babies- there's nothing you can lose,
Big stretchy frames and they're not station mated,
And if you get them I'll guarantee you'll be elated.

You all know what they're worth but I'll suggest a figure,
Do I hear five pounds to get me on my way?
I know you've plenty of heart but show me a little vigour,
Five pound's not too much for the best sheep here today.

Thank you sir – I'm bid five pounds- bid five bid five,
And I'll take a shilling to keep this sale alive,
Do I hear five pounds one for these beautifully presented sheep?
And you all know at five pounds they're going far too cheap!

Thank you sir I'm bid five pounds one- now make that two,
Five three I'm bid now five four – bid four bid four I'm bid four,
Five pounds five I'm bid five bid five I'm bid five guineas for one ewe,
And you all know they're worth at least another ten bob more!

How many in the pen Dud? What, six hundred and fifty two?
And I'm only bid five guineas for a perfectly bred young ewe?
These ewes can be yours to join when and how you choose,
So why are you holding back? What do you have to lose?

I'm bid five pounds six – now seven – bid seven I'm bid seven deniers,
Eight-bid five pounds eight shillings-nine- I'm bid nine bid nine,
They're on the market! And I'm only bid five pounds nine for a pen of weaners,
Now one more bid might get them sir, is your star ready to shine?

Now I'll defy anyone here to judge these sheep to a shilling!
And you're in the box seat sir, you can seal the deal if you're willing?
Ten-I'm bid five pounds ten shillings, and I'm going to knock them,
I'm bid ten bid ten and there's no way I'm gonna hock 'em!

I'm bid five and a half quid and this is my last and final call?
Sold! Congratulations Sir– and I dips me lid with regards,
You sure know your sheep and these ewes will make you a haul,
 Because they're the best young ewes ever to grace these yards!"

The Nomadic Enigma

He drifted in and joined our group and soon became an enigma,
It was clear to all concerned that he was a nomadic stray,
But either untouched or totally undaunted by any stigma,
Cos all doubts we may have had he was able to allay.

We believe he came to us, quite simply, just by chance,
Through the bread ministry we use to nourish the poor,
And day by day as he worked with us his status did enhance,
Because as we come to know him we admired him even more

He was always clean shaven and very neatly attired,
And not once did he say a word you'd construe to offend,
And we learned from his habits that towards sobriety he aspired,
And thus we come to regard him, quite warmly as a friend.

But regarding his past, he religiously remained tight lipped,
Though well educated there seemed to be no doubt,
Because his vocabulary was very well equipped,
When speaking on current issues and especially on matters devout

Now age is a contentious issue, but we figured he'd be round fifty,
Although his appearance for a stray, was truly well preserved,
And that would indicate he is a recent nomadic drifty,
And before joining us, he held a position in which he served.

He refused to be drawn on any past employment,

Stating firmly "look, I'm here to attempt a new start",
So we withdrew queries about his previous work deployment,
To help him settle in and assist him to play his part

But of course that didn't stop us from engaging in conjecture,
And we wondered, could he have been a teacher in our schools?
Or perhaps at a university, where he would give a lecture?
Cos his hands indicated he hadn't worked with tools.

Was it possible he was a lawyer before joining with our crew?
Or did he hold down a cushy job, within the public service?
But then, he could so easily have been an accountant too,
Or maybe a male nurse, because nothing made him nervous.

Who knows, he may have served in our countries policing force,
Or employed in a bank, and been the manager there at least,
But, regarding others' misfortunes, he always showed remorse,
So we all asked ourselves– could he have been a Parish Priest?

Because he showed great compassion for his fellow man,
Often rendering service in lieu of his own health,
While every morning he attended Mass (with the local clan)
And he showed scant respect for accumulating wealth!

Whatever he'd been previously was never there on show,
Or if it was, well, we were just too dumb to convince,
But whatever it was he did, I guess now we'll never really know,
Cos one morning he was gone, and we haven't seen him since!

Derby

Derby is a pretentious name, but it was the one bestowed upon our horse,
Whose genes trace back to trotting stock, according to our source,
And as a farm hack he was broken to saddle and was so easily ridden,
But when yoked to a sulky he'd display traits that were otherwise hidden.

He is brown in colour, quiet by nature and stands fourteen and a half hands high
But on every inch of that rangy frame you knew you could rely.
He dislikes being caught in the paddock and will lead you a merry dance,
As round and round the field he'd gallop and buck and prance.

He is a very intelligent steed, and his horse sense often proves productive,
Cos when he detects a trip to town, he can really become obstructive.
Just harness him in the sulky then take the road to town,
And you can bet your bottom dollar he's going to let you down!

Once the penny drops and he's sure of his detection,
He will slow and jib and the sulky ceases in all forward projection.
And it does not matter how you react– you can plead with him and cajole,
He'll get determined, and refuse to allow those sulky wheels to roll!

If you turn him round he'll take off like the proverbial Bondi tram,
And that proves there is nothing wrong (it's only a horsey scam)
But once you reverse him round again in an effort to head for town,
He'll slow right down and stop – and I'm darned if you can talk him roun'!

Derby trained with the Light Horse Brigade – he and my eldest brother,
But Derby was discharged cos he lacked the temperament of all the other
Cos he is a farmer's nag and loves peace and quiet and lacks the urge to travel,
And he can become quite obsessive, if this starts to unravel

The Spotlight Shooters

A voice called frantically "fire a shot to veer him",
And the fox whirled at right angles,
And now his naked body dangles,
If he'd reached the fence there's no way we'd have gotten near him,
But the fox turned and was fatally shot,
And it was my Dad who engineered the plot.
So our lambs and chooks have no further need to fear him.

"There's a dull red glow two hundred yards to our rear,
So keep alert- I'll bet it's the fox's mate!
She's unaware of the old dogs' fate,
So keep the noise down or you'll drive her off in fear,
We'll let her settle for minute or three,
And then I'll flash the light and see what we can see,
Cos we're at the fence and we don't want her coming near.

When he switched the light on and began to reconnoitre,
The fox had drifted down the field,
So to the group he anxiously appealed,
"Start the motor and begin pursuit- there's no further need to loiter",
Cos by now the fox was up and running,
With the spot lighters in pursuit and gunning,
But their aim was as effective as someone stricken with a goitre.

The fox had made a beeline for some scrub not so far away,
A shot was fired to enticed the fox to turn,

But some shooters will never really learn,
They forgot to factor in velocity and the speed of a fleeing prey,
Cos they all fired at the speeding fox,
 But the pellets landed behind its hocks,
And that lucky animal continued to lead them all astray.

It was my Dad sitting warm and cosy next the driver in the front,
Who finally drew the fatal bead,
That filled the vixen full of lead,
And his retort to fellow shooters seemed terse and rather blunt,
Go home and learn to shoot,
If you want to bag some loot,
And then perhaps we can organise another spotlight hunt.

Spot light shooting can be a dangerous, yet an exhilarating sport,
If you obey each and every rule,
And do not play the fool.
Cos the eye glows from animals differ- so do take time to sort,
Between the rabbit and the hare,
And the cats and possums there,
To save many from demise when they're not the prey you sought!

The Bidgee Flood

We were marking calves when the official word came through,
Phoned in by the controller – that the Bidgee had over grew,
Be prepared for the biggest flood since that of seventy four,
But more rain could make it even larger than we've ever seen before!
So we boosted up our revs as went up a gear or two,
And finished marking the calves without any more ado

We had two days before the waters would come and inundate,
Some portions of our land, two days for us to anticipate,
How far the water will expand, and how long it may remain.
We had two whole days to curse the woes of flooding rain.
But, tis the law of our land, tis either a famine or a feast,
And we can leave it or expand, or hang in there at least.

The muddy swirling waters came and spread out 'ore our lea,
And all fences in its path got damaged, or even washed away.
Later we got a crop of Bathurst burr left there by the flood,
And we wrestled with the curse of Paterson stranded in the mud,
 I believe we got our share of the famous Gundagai thistle,
That grew so thick it removed the desire to even want to whistle.

Eventually we sprayed out the weeds and fixed up all our fences,
And readied for the next one (cos you never think of floods in past tenses)
But we're not done, we just keep on farming and living in expectation,

Of the day when the controller calls to warn of another infiltration,
Of a new Bidgee flow, together with those things it seems to encumber.
Til then we'll mosey along, cos by now we've been through quite a number!

Perty Cat

The day we met I was preoccupied on the internet,
When this mournful meow came drifting down the hall.
And when I opened up the door I was unable to ignore,
The Siamese cat squatting there, so regal and so tall

Although emaciated she immediately had me fascinated,
Because as felines go she was a beauty queen,
She's been here before Julie told and she's growing bold,
As she responds to my viands routine

I ventured out but she was full of fear and doubt
And sought refuge underneath my car,
A bowl of tasty trout enticed the young pussy out
But one false step and she was ready to run afar

But as time evolved she became more resolved
To trust in our reception
She was an outdoor cat and unprepared to surrender that
But dined indoors with no exception

But at night when fierce thunder rent the sky asunder,
She'd be there, meowing at our door
And to appease her fright she'd often stay all night
Or until those rumblings she was able to ignore

She developed a strict routine surrounding her daily cuisine,

And her first meal began at five thirty each day
She loved the menu at her seemingly favourite venue
But when finished refused to stay

But she would show appreciation with her undying adulation
That was so hard to ignore
She would purr and cast her spell and do it oh so well
Before heading toward the door

And once you let her out she would carefully look about
Considering where to start
And when I'd leave for work she bid goodbye and then lurk
Beside a shrub and watch me depart

Now this was the daily scene, every day the same routine
For the two years she lived with us
Not once did she deviate so it was easy to anticipate
Her location, and not be left nonplus

This morning began quite normal, with Perty acting formal
And adhering to her strict routine
She enjoyed her meal and then considered the time ideal
To merge into the outdoor scene

I attended to my ablutions with my mind upon solutions
Regarding my daily chores
Then I donned my attire which only seemed to inspire
A desire to get outdoors

But there was Perty Cat sitting there upon the mat
And begging to return,
So I took her back inside for a second helping to provide,
But for this she did not yearn.
It was my attention she desired and refused to be denied,

And begged with me to share
Now I didn't want to offend but I had a job to attend,
And I had a need to be there.

She followed me across the floor as I departed thru the door,
With her trying to deter
I was already running late when I finally opened up the gate
Despite Perty's guile and purr

Her behaviour was the complete reverse and getting even worse
Then she'd ever displayed before
She clearly wanted me to stay and this only led to my dismay
As I approached my car door

Then when seated down inside and as the gear stick I applied
I heard a sad and mournful cry
She was there at my door and with her blue eyes did implore
Me not to pass her by

I knew something wasn't right but couldn't figure out the plight
So I reversed onto the street
She followed me to our gate then sadly watched me accelerate
While I left her there discrete

Now when I returned at night Perty was nowhere there in sight
And she always gave a reception
So I went and searched around but she was nowhere to be found,
And all this was beyond our perception

Was her safety being sought and she'd needed my support
And I'd ignored her?
Or had her nomadic lust returned and parting had her concerned,
And caused her to deter?

I know Perty was severely stressed and only wanted to be caressed
And I up and departed
Although we loved the time we shared and to it nothing can be compared
 We now find ourselves parted.

She came to us from out of the blue with her friendship loyal and true
To win our hearts
But now she has gone away, leaving those hearts as heavy as clay,
To some unknown parts

Perty's behaviour that morning beset us without any warning
And why we can only guess
But we miss you terribly Perty Cat and not knowing where you're at
Is the reason why we stress.

Friendships come and friendships go and only some are destined to grow
While others fail to germinate
We valued the friendship Perty brought and her absence leaves us all distraught
But we do have memories, to celebrate.

Yeah, I Can Remember

Yeah, I do remember the floods of nineteen thirty nine,
Following a terrible drought with features non-benign
And even tho I was only five,
There are certain things I remember oh so well
How the creeks gently flowed before they began to quickly swell
Even before the rains reached overdrive!

My Dad enlarged a dry dam just downstream from our home
And built a wall across the creek by using the excavated loam
But then it worried him
Cos he never dreamed of torrential rains or seeing the waters peak,
Or being threatened with home invasion by the placid Yaven Creek
But it haunted him

Our homestead was isolated by the rising water when we retired that night
Our house was cosy inside and we thought everything would be alright,
But our sleep-out took in water.
Cos it was ankle deep on the floorboards when we scrambled out next morning,
And later in the day the wall collapsed without a sign of warning,
And water drained from our bricks and mortar

The Walsh's were our upstream neighbours and greeted this news with a huge hooray,

Because water was barely inches away from their mud-brick house of clay,
Cos they owned a pisi homestead,
And they were an hour away from water invasion when the relief was heaven sent,
Because the family had been on full alert for several days without relent,
But now they have a future instead

The extremities of those floodwaters were created by human hand
But way back then I was far too young to fully understand
But I pursued the subject later in life
And I now posthumously apologise to my Dad for disclosing his misdeed
Cos he didn't visualise the consequences, he only wanted the plan to succeed
And had no wish to cause any strife

My Dad had a vision to store water but had no meaningful consultation
And the final projected water levels were never taken into calculation
Cos a surveyor was not consulted
Our home was at the junction of two creeks and when the water finally receded
It would have been left completely isolated had the outrageous plan succeeded
It was in the planning, my Father faulted

The stored water would have severed family access to town, front and rear
And this was one of many abnormalities that began suddenly to appear
And our house could flood again!

And one of the most disruptive features would have seen our farm cut in half
And this should have been addressed in planning, not left for the aftermath
Sorry Pater, but the facts are plain!

The moral to this story is, never oppose nature in the belief that you will succeed
Research your projects carefully because if you don't Nature will supersede
And there'll be egg on your face
Yes, be adventurous but stay conventional, and do not rely solely on your heart
Allow for the might of nature in your projects, and never plan to outsmart
And success may become yours, with God's grace.

Grace And Understanding – Where Art Thou Gone?

We are undergoing tremendous change in this modern society
And compared with yesteryear we've been exposed to an avalanche of variety
We seniors have never experienced liberty of this magnitude before
But we do get confused by those conversing in their latest dialogue
So much so they say and do things that leave many of us agog
While grace and understanding of peers, we simply ignore

Parents' advised their juveniles as they forged their way in life
To never utter hurtful words to intentionally stir up strife
Respect the down trodden, cos for the grace of God it could be you
I recall how we adored our spiritual leaders and held them in awe
Now a group want to control the clergy, and are causing much rancour,
Hearken, oh grace and understanding, your presence is over-due.

Grace is what we need when we're out presenting God
And understanding is an asset to give another's view the nod
But are they still compatible with the vocabulary so many have adopted?
We see aggression in our genders and the belief they were born to lead
And they confess their love for Jesus but are not living out His creed
Oh Grace and Understanding, your traits need to be co-opted!

I can hearken back to yesteryear and recall with great delight
How our pews were always full, even on Sunday night
When Grace and Understanding were our cornerstones for worship
We respected our spiritual leader and didn't query symbolic content
We supported and upheld, and left the Clergy to preach, and present
But Grace and Understanding, that was when we valued your fellowship.

So what is driving our egos to turn our backs on understanding grace?
Is it peer pressure, or simply a challenge for our vanity to embrace?
Grace and understanding are drawcards, a fact that nobody will deny
So why not support convention instead of arguing to get our own way?
Do we no longer pray to God, and our pride and ego demand the final say?
Oh come, Grace and Understanding, have we really passed you by?

We'll grow closer to God's heart with grace than we ever will with animosity
And people always heed when presented with compassion and generosity
Our Lord is a loving Lord and would delight to see these traits in you
So let's change our ways of thinking and get rid of that aggression
Cos we have all the elements we need right here in our possession,
Yes, Grace and Understanding and we all know, what they can do!

Women Of Distinction

The males of our community are on notice, and need to be aware
All controlling rights in governance they will now have to share
As our lady counterparts mount a true and just claim
For roles in leadership which they so justly can proclaim

We have a lady Premier presenting proposals in State Caucus
And she remains calm and collected when the opposition are raucous
She sets the standards for feminine leadership with great recourse
So if you seek direction, efficiency and grace, women are your source

The Wagga Uniting Church Council have appointed a lady at its head
And the congregation is not lamenting, they're all rejoicing now instead
Because she is a very gracious lady, and is battle wise and can get tough
As well as fair, just and encouraging, and knows when enough is enough.

And the Presbytery sent a Minister who belongs to the feminine gender
To aide in planning proposals with a need for her to render
All matters thrown her way she handles with the greatest poise
Cos she radiates so much confidence with the skills that she employs

History is being created in Wagga, with two female Clerics now appointed
And for the first time there's no male preacher currently anointed
And the congregation is ecstatic with not a single defaulter
Now these clerics are destined for church folklore as our rocks of Gibraltar

If you venture into the Admin Centre you'll get a cheery greeting
Because the lady there inspires and takes a heck of a lot of beating
When it comes to courtesy and grace and issuing a great reception
Cos all her skills towards admin and management have no exception

These ladies were not appointed by default, but entirely on their merit
 And this is a history making era and I'm so glad I'm here to share it
But I know another mission that would create tremendous hope
And that is if one day they decided to name a lady Pope.

Seek Ye The Grace Of God

I've strolled by pools of still waters,
In the bosom of the Yavern Creek,
And I've trodden on fields of lush green clover,
And tended herds so shiny, round and sleek,
And when recalling the words of Psalm twenty three,
It made me feel oh so thankful and so meek.

But don't expect to always bask in sunshine,
There'll be shadows through which we must traverse
But we can stave off evil when we seek the grace of God
And watch the clouds in the valleys as they disperse
Fear no harm, but be comforted by the Lord and His staff,
When we support Him as our Saviour of this universe

The Lord prepares a path for us, and surely we can follow,
Despite our adversaries the Lord will anoint our heads with oil,
Then our cups of happiness and well being will start to overflow
Goodness and love will pursue us all our days if we are loyal
And choose to stay with the Lord forever and obey only He
But we need to remain sincere – because only we can foil.

In this modern era we think we're sophisticated and smart,
But we are confronted by far too many choices,
And we seldom hear the Word of the Lord,
Because it's so often drowned by the din of other voices
And you'll rarely find a soul with the intestinal fortitude

To stand up and say "I'm following Jesus", and then rejoices.

Yesteryear

Of all the functions I've attended and thoroughly enjoyed the most,
This one excited me more and stirred my memory so,
And I refer to my school reunion where I really had a ball,
When I sat and talked with friends from that so era long ago.

We swapped many tales (and I'm sure embellished a few)
And I suspect created one or two especially for the day,
But after the show had closed I couldn't help myself,
From recalling other bits that occurred along the way

I well recall the first day I rode my bike to school,
Along Pamandi Road that I shared with my sister Ruth.
And the terror I felt when the first whistle blew haunts me e'en to day,
When I first took my place in line as a super data sleuth,

The enrolment totalled sixteen – with me at the foot of the ladder,
So when Laurie started I thought this is the end of that,
Cos it was my turn to climb the ladder and I let young Laurie know,
But I guess I was too cocky cos it riled his brother Pat!

I unwittingly exposed myself to a flaw in my repertoire.
By not monitoring the outcome ' ore doing what I 'orter",
So I took a crash course in biology (tho I really knew the answer!)
Cos sibling blood's much thicker than any plain old water!

I relished the lessons including the triple Rs,
And enjoyed great rapport as I ascended the pecking ladder,
Cos the needs for which developing minds all strive,
Is peer acceptance which will make your heart feel gladder.

Sportsmanship and graciousness were on our schools agenda,
We were taught to play hard and fair but always strive to a win,
And modesty was a must if we ended up the victor,
But losing wasn't hard when accepted with a grin.

I recalled the day Horrie sent a note that he was feeling crook
"please go home and return tomorrow when your lessons will resume".
Now we were just a bunch of kids with no teacher there in charge?
Out in the sticks, no supervision, and free of the old school room?

We were in no hurry and we hit on a splendid plan!
Why not race our bicycles? Right there on Pamandi Road?
It was a dream and all went well before that cry of alarm!
Horrie was espied in fullest flight as towards the school he strode!

We still had time to hide or even make a dash for home!
But we had grit and decided to stay and cop it sweet!
But there were doubts when we saw Horrie's mouth edged in foam,
And without preamble he duly cancelled our very first bicycle meet.

He granted bail and sent us home tho we knew there'd be more to come!
And after a rush we reduced our speed as we drew nearer our selection,
We thought it wise to arrive on time and with just a slice of luck,
After Mother's greeting we might escape any closer detection.

The next morning dawned cloudless, deleting the chance of remission,
School was our destiny unless we could find stay of execution!
We offered to forgo studies and help our sire mark his lambs,
But he declined our offer by granting us full absolution!

Back at the school our bravado gone in the wake of uncertainty,
And our peer support was low tho' now it was badly needed!
Cos that usual peer allegiance was nowhere to be seen,
Just remorse for that teacher's note – and the fact it wasn't heeded!

Horrie was on time and smiled and nodded with his usual show of affection,
But we weren't dumb – we knew how appearances can deceive!
And later his agenda became known as we were duly informed,
Four cuts to our hands is what we would all receive!

Memories can be jigsaw puzzles – they commence when you are born,
And each year we add a little til we conclude our pictorial plan,
And when the difficult bits are in place it leaves time for us to enjoy,
So why hurry? Let's take our time – as we complete our natural span

The Food Chain

We were very alert as we reversed into the loading dock.
But we had one eye glued on the Market's outside clock,
Although we well aware we had the Super Marts permission,
We also knew we barely had a minute left to spare
Before the Market would be expecting us to be there,
To collect the produce they'd reserved for our mission.

We normally collect thirteen bestowals every single week
But that collection can increase when donations tend to peak
We do encourage gardeners to donate all of their residuals,
And when they begin reaping their freshly grown product
We will then collect their surplus with responsible conduct,
And those collections we then distribute to deserving individuals

We received a call from a High School, a regular donator,
And were offered a load of Queensland blues and several more,
We arrived for the pickup and were met by the duty class,
And they began to load my car, and piled it to the brim
They were a friendly group that scanned from obese to very slim.
And were full of fun and mischief, but we chose to allow it all to pass!

We rang the distributor to learn if their milk supply was excessive,
And the Boss was cool but his vocals were becoming little expressive,
He said he had a Ute load with its use by date expiring,

It was trash, but it was destined to become someone else's treasure,
Cos we were able to give it away without imposing any measure,
It's a frustrating occupation at times, but it can also be inspiring!

It can become humiliating, sitting and waiting to pick up bread,
Some know why we are there and will pause to pat us on the head,
But then some older ladies think we're only there to perve,
There's temptation, but our motivation has long ago been spent,
And we allow the colourful parade to pass, without recognition or comment,
Besides, the collections require all the energies we've stored up in reserve!

When we were allowed to collect the different types of bread and various rolls
We returned to base to slice and wrap before giving them out to deserving souls,
And that is nothing new we have been doing it now for almost twenty years,
And we still try to present it in orderly fashion, so our clients can quickly choose.
While we stand and supervise, and watch as they all methodically peruse.
It's not a skilful task and we remain polite, and always treat them as our peers.

Different nationalities representing many cultures, all form our clientele,
And despite their many differences and languages, they get along so very well,
With only one or two exceptions, fuelled by their own ignorance and greed,
But we are focused on being fair and just and are only there to cater for,

And to welcome all of them, as they venture through our door. However, there is a need to remain vigilant for this mission to succeed.

The Trappers

We elected to ride our bike, rather than commit to a lengthy hike,
When laying down our traps for the night,
Because we went out trapping hares that usually dwell in pairs,
Even when exposed to the summits might.

Hares are devoted as a pair, and under the cloak of night will always share,
Their feeding times together,
Then at dawn each returns to a squat, and remains there even when it's hot,
Or during any change in the weather,

And when you find out where they exit fences, then you are weakening their defences,
Because you'll know the portal where they getaway,
It's important that your traps cover this outlet, so you will be in control from the outset
And I am unaware of any better way.

Now when you're out there trapping rabbits, with their domesticated habits,
You'll need to adopt a different ploy
If you're wondering where they'll be found then seek for their community underground,
It's there they find the safety they enjoy.

They choose to live underground in a warren, and to rabbits this is not at all foreign,

It's the safest place they know,
But they all venture out at night, because they can penetrate darkness with their sight,
But any exposure to lights will cause their eyes to glow.

Now where should I set my traps when I want to capture these small chaps?
I know their numbers are becoming vast,
Well set your traps at the entrance where they reside, or wherever else you may decide,
Because their habitats expand so fast,

What do you do when trapping foxes? Without a doubt they are the most obnoxious,
And I detest what it is they entail
If you have an old dead chook, throw it on an open fire and allow it to partly cook
Then use it, to lay an inviting trail

Just drag it along the earthen face until you're convinced you've found the ideal place,
And you partly bury the bait,
But make sure your traps are underground, arranged so the chook they all surround,
Then sit back, relax and wait.

Whenever you go out trapping prey you'll encroach on an area regarded as grey,
By many of the local populace,
And when a species reaches plague proportions, opinions expressed will have lots of distortions,
And will need to be tempered with some grace
Mass baiting will eradicate the species you desire, but its agonising, and other species will expire,

And it's not at all humane
Whereas trapping allows for discrimination, and only the species chosen face elimination
And all other species will remain.

The Evolution Of Youth

I used to love driving in my Ford and together with my two mates all on board,
We would often sing our hearts out,
But late one Sunday afternoon it gave up the ghost, like a deflated balloon,
We were twenty miles from home and all plagued with doubt.

There was a link missing from the carburettor, and our plight was not becoming any better,
So we foraged around and found some wire,
And with a pair of pliers in hand we fashioned a link from just one single strand
And then towards mechanical dynamics we began to aspire.

Five years later that link was still installed, and the Ford was keeping us all enthralled,
But our singing had become a little more composed,
And then other pursuits attracted our attention, some of which we shall not even mention,
And we found ourselves often indisposed.

Now during those long summer weekends we were sometimes home and at loose ends,
Cos it was in winter we played our footy, God bless,
But on Saturday nights we'd all go dancing, and even tried our hands at romancing,
But it originated no success.

As time progressed so did our maturity, and we thought more of our future and security,
And less of the care free days of yore
Although my Ford was still a sound rig, I retired it but searched for a reason to renege,
But I truly knew it would not be needed any more.

Because we had all married and settled down, be it in different parts and another town,
And our paths were destined never to cross again.
But I visualise us lads together in my Ford, singing out of tune but never ever bored,
But now, only one of us remain

We always planned to have a reunion, but circumstances denied us that communion,
Because my two best mates both passed away,
So if you know something you think worth doing, get on with it and start hotly pursuing,
And still able do it while you may!

Stubble Reduction

I contacted our local Shire Councillor for a permit to burn our wheaten stubble,
And it was granted providing we observed regulations to avoid creating undue trouble,
We had to notify our neighbours and ensure the water cart occupied prime space,
And prior to burning off make certain all our ploughed fire breaks were in place.

We were allocated a time to ignite and this with other directions we carefully observed, Because it was a serious undertaking so we paid it the strict attention it deserved,
We first ignited the eastern boundary after factoring in a gentle westerly breeze,
And after a couple of passes with a fire harrow we created the safety break to appease.

It was then we dragged the fire harrow all around the edge of that stubbled field,
Then watched as the flames danced in fury, fuelled by residue from the previous yield
And although it was a controlled burn its ferocity left us stricken there with awe
And fully supporting rules and regulations, and ready to follow every letter of the law.

Fire can become a very valuable asset, but its potential must also be respected,
Because a spark can cause a raging inferno, so all fires must never be neglected,
Fire can also be a handy tool, but it needs to be harnessed and closely controlled,
And when you burn unwanted refuse those burning fires must always be patrolled.

When a fire turns feral and leaps the boundary, the damage caused can be astronomical,
And all rural enterprises within its path, can be totally rendered uneconomical,
But farmers regroup, in spite of grants and discounts and comprehensive insurance,
And rebuild, while a question mark may linger over the longevity of their endurance.

We had an amazing burn, paying attention to burning protocol and all its relevant actions,
But we were forever vigilant, guarding against interference from other outside factions.
We had our cleanest burn ever, and there was not a single issue to cause us any concern,
And for this we were extremely grateful to our Lord, and gave Him our thanks in return.

God – Our Leader

Many church folk posses this aim, to be able serve others in God's name
But often find it hard to endue
Because even when we try, it so often becomes super hard to deny,
Our wills from ruling what we do.

Church folk impress when given the nod, until their egos begin replacing God,
And personalities need to have a rein,
But our God is here to lead and without Him it's doubtful we'll succeed
It's only when we follow that we gain.

Two wrongs will never make a right so let us seek to find the real true light,
And let God lead our way,
We are meant to be our Lord's servant so let us become more observant,
And heed what He has to say.

If you think He's a screen of smoke then you'd better find another bloke,
Cos God is as genuine as they come,
Follow Him and never be led astray, and commit to Him in every other way,

And it'll feel like coming home.

He'll teach us all about godliness and grace that we'll find so easy to embrace,
When we learn about Christianity on the go,
And He'll encourage and He'll guide us, without further ado and undue fuss,
As in His faith we grow.

God's people are willing to welcome you, even when old or very new,
To Christianity,
And they'll welcome you as family, and will help us all to settle happily,
And help in appeasing vanity.

Our Lord Jesus is the real true light, and if it's from darkness you seek respite,
Then you need to follow God,
God's doctrine will show all of us the way if we only follow what He has to say
Because He remains our Staff and Rod,

If you've sinned and feel very discontent, follow God's doctrine and start to repent,
Cos He is a very forgiving Lord,
His advice will help you mend your ways, and following Him will render better days,
And you'll feel real glad to be on board.

God can deliver us from all evil, He can also protect when life faces an upheaval,
If you trust Him with all your heart,

Now it is not an old maid's story, God possesses all the power and the glory,
And when you believe, all this He'll impar

The True Meaning Of Christmas

Christmas bells and decorations form the basis for different types of celebrations,
And all on Christmas day,
Jesus birth and the wisdom of prophets versus commercialisation and corporate profits,
And we can choose the way!

At Yuletide Christians will thank God in church, for all the confidence and grace they search
And this has become their traditional way,
While non-Christians not prone to being overwrought, will not spare Him a single thought,
And worship ale and victuals on the day,

Others lavish their children with rare gifts, and the more expensive, greater seem their lifts
And they never dream of thanking the Lord of hosts,
They ask, what has He ever done for us? And just can't understand why all Christians fuss,
And are more inclined to believe the reign of ghosts

Some never acquire Christmas decorations to install, or use Christmas slogans to enthral,
But simply disregard Christmas day.
They detest those who belong to a Christian society, especially if they display religious piety,

And refuse to regard them in any single way.

Christ was born of the Virgin Mary, whom Herod for one would have loved to bury,
But Christ was born to be our Chief,
Displaying these qualities while just a Kid until later He was confronted by a guileful bid
Until His human reign ended up in grief,

But our illustrious leader was not outdone, He rose from the dead as our Lord's Son,
Thus confirming what the prophets all had said,
Jesus emerged from His sacred crypt, full of divine spirituality and much better equipped,
To foretell all that lay ahead.

Christmas moods will often seize us, and urge us to celebrate the birth of Jesus,
While other motives are often excessive,
Because there is no other valid reason, for celebrating at this time of the season,
And when Christians can be expressive

If you have belief then there's nothing to debate, but how can non-believers ever relate,
To the reason for their revel, If Jesus is a lie, then why do they have a fete? What is it they and their children celebrate?
And let's hope, it's not inspired by the devil!

Our Anninersary

We've celebrated one hundred and fifty years of worship in our church,
One hundred and fifty years of faithfulness and love,
One hundred and fifty years of Bible study and research,
With the last thirty seven inspired by the encircled cross and dove.

Our ancestors laid foundations those many long years ago,
Foundations lovingly added to as the years have sped along,
And though our work is incomplete with fertile fields to sow,
We celebrate our anniversary with prayerful thanks and song.

We have noticed many changes as down the years we scroll.
How many came in sulkies and some used shank's mare,
And all were exposed to elements like rain and heat and cold,
While today's transport is air conditioned and quite extraordinaire.

Now the women wore their very best all buttoned to the chin,
And hats and gloves and stockings completed their dress attire,
And a heavy suit and hat and tie is what the men dressed in,
Yet despite the heat and no air conditioning no one did expire.

Today we dress more casually yet some their modesty have abused,
The ladies hats and gloves have gone and some dresses are revealing,

And the men only wear suits for special do's and ties are seldom used,
And we all like these changes, in fact most are quite appealing.

After one hundred and fifty years- where do we go from here?
Our members are growing older and the pews are becoming vacant,
Yet new members from the masses seem reluctant to appear,
So is there need for subtle change – or is that a little blatant?

We must never interfere with our Holy Bible's DNA,
It is the Word of God and its authenticity is eternal,
But how it's presented will need to change along the way,
If we want younger folk to enter when they pass by our external!

Changes are raging all around us while we remain steeped in our traditions,
Traditions that overflowed our churches not so many years ago,
But those customs no longer guarantee membership additions,
And we owe it to our Lord to help our churches live and grow.

You and I love our present customs – but our contracts are expiring,
And many of our home grown family seldom worship any more,
So do we need to revise our customs and make worship more inspiring,
For the younger generation, when they venture through our door?

The Emmaus Team

A jovial team from Emmaus rolled into Bimbadeen,
For intensive training with hearts focussed on perfection,
But they were realistic and knew the risks involved,
Where-ever the devil lurks he majors in deflection'

Because he tempted many with his stay at home offers,
Of warmth and comfort and late rising from their bed,
And his promise of no pressure and no need for any talks,
Can be tempting when allowed space within your head.

But the lure of Christian fellowship, and a chance to serve our Lord,
Is all that Christians need to warm their hearts and souls,
Because a sincere Christian will choose the Lord every single time,
And will reject the devil when he tries to kick some goals.

Now this lot from Emmaus is a group to behold,
Each were called so the Lord could use their talent,
And they didn't ask why or query the wisdom used,
They were content to be there, ready, willing and gallant.

An amazing group who can give and take the mickey,
Because some have been at it since they were just a teen,
Is it the way they mix their banter with their humour,
And their love for the Lord, that they were called to Bimbadeen?

Now only a few are musical, but all can sing their faith,
And with great gusto too, tho some are better than others,
But all of them posses a deep love for their Lord,
And are willing to share it with sisters and brothers

After all these years some things I know for certain,
Like the Lord demands our trust, but has no call to obey us,
But if ever I were caught down there in the trenches,
Who would I want with me? That team form Emmaus

The Apprentice Sheaf Turner

"Now listen to what I say
And we'll get along fine today"
The Builder was the Boss of the crew
And the sheaf turner was a rookie brand new
The Boss had built many stacks throughout a career
That spanned several years and he stood alone without a peer
While the rookie was in his first job -and wanting to learn the ropes
The Boss is in need of a good sheaf turner and the job will be his if he copes
"Now loosen up lad-we'll mosey along, lay the foundation and get it tidy and straight
Then it will be time to up the tempo a tad, and give this baby some life, can you handle it mate?"
Although the rookie was as keen as mustard he knew full well with a brand new boss you dare not diddle
Now there were some who reckoned the rookie was a little thick, well that maybe so- but only through the middle
"I'll tell you now my lad this is what I want to see you do- to start with I want the sheaves all butts first placed out in front
And I don't want to see you playing the Smart Alec and start placing them behind me bum where I need to turn around and grunt
Now I do like to see them coming nice and fast and even but don't you dare ever attempt to chuck them on the sheaf already on my fork
And I want you keep your mind right on your work – and keep your trap shut tight – and concentrate-I don't want to even hear you try to talk
Now just one more thing before we get ourselves underway, I want you to be very careful with the fork you have and please do not offend
And think it smart and trendy to waive it in the breeze like a piece of dirty rag– why, their prongs a very sharp and are also deadly friend"
The young rookie paid strict attention and followed out all his instructions but that did not stop the builder from indulging in some sport
But the rookie sheaf turner's instinct urged him to keep his mouth shut but he would have loved to have replied with an odd retort
His hands became so sore and blistered but not once did he complain although instead he decided he would wear a pair of gloves
Now some of his fellow workers said he was a sissy, and he was tempted into retaliation with his fork with a few gentle shoves
But he had mentally compounded while he was also physically expanding and he gradually earned his peers' respect overall
They had originally predicted he wouldn't last a week but he was tough, hard and had stamina and was able to stand tall
And when the final haystack had been completed and they all gathered round to celebrate and to share friendly talk
The rookie began to sing "round and round the haystack like a grizzly bear, heads first, butts first, and with a fork
I was often tempted to tickle the Boss's great backside - only of course to see how well it was she danced"
The young rookie chortled with gleeful confidence and exuberance, but somewhat artificially enhanced
By the cheer he consumed because for the first time in his life he now considered himself a man
Because of the spirit in which his workmates accepted him as a valued member of their clan

ABOUT THE AUTHOR

Although he'll probably deny it, he does possess a certain expertise in his dealings with people. He does enjoy writing also, but he has never had anything published previously. He believes most people can relate to the word battling, so he thinks it is appropriate to call his book "Just Battlin' On Regardless".

www.ingramcontent.com/pod-product-compliance
Lightning Source LLC
Chambersburg PA
CBHW061306110426
42742CB00012BA/2075